LAND ASSESSMENT IN SCOTLAND

LAND ASSESSMENT IN SCOTLAND

Proceedings of the
ROYAL SCOTTISH GEOGRAPHICAL SOCIETY SYMPOSIUM
held in the University of Edinburgh
on 25 May 1979

Edited on behalf of the Society by

M F THOMAS

Professor of Earth and Environmental Science
University of Stirling

and

J T COPPOCK

Ogilvie Professor of Geography
University of Edinburgh

Aberdeen University Press

First published 1980
© M F Thomas and J T Coppock 1980

British Library Cataloguing in Publication Data
Land assessment in Scotland
1. Land use, Rural—Scotland—Congresses
I. Thomas, Michael Frederic
II. Coppock, John Terence
III. Royal Scottish Geographical Society
333.7'6'09411   HD618
ISBN 0-08-025716-X

PRINTED IN GREAT BRITAIN
THE UNIVERSITY PRESS
ABERDEEN

CONTENTS

FIGURES

TABLES

PREFACE

This volume of papers and discussion arises out of a symposium, organised by the editors on behalf of the Royal Scottish Geographical Society and held in the University of Edinburgh on 25th May 1979. The theme of Land Assessment in Scotland was chosen in order to focus attention on a wide range of problems associated with the present and possible future uses of mainly rural land. The selection of topics has been restricted to appraisals of the natural environment, and there is an emphasis, not wholly intended, on the problems of Scottish uplands.

The editors were conscious from the beginning that many different organisations are currently concerned with these questions, and that their priorities differ markedly, and occasionally conflict. The importance of bringing their work into focus now is that many government bodies are actively engaged in consultations and/or in the development of new programmes of data collection and manipulation. But no organisation has overall responsibility for deciding future policy in terms of the methodology of land assessment or the allocation of resources to programmes of land classification and evaluation, and no comprehensive review has been undertaken of the different techniques presently employed by existing organisations or available to them.

The symposium was therefore offered as a forum for the expression and exchange of views on these matters, and it is hoped that the wider publication of the papers and discussions will encourage further consultation and stimulate scientific enquiry into problems associated with land assessment in Scotland in which no single interest can be regarded as having an overriding priority in this discussion. The volume also demonstrates the diversity of land uses for which assessment may be required in an advanced country.

ACKNOWLEDGMENTS

The editors wish to thank all the organisations represented in this volume for agree-
ing so readily to take part in the Symposium and to have their papers published and
for providing illustrative materials.   They would also like to thank Dr. A.J. Crosbie
Chairman of the Department of Geography, University of Edinburgh, for his assistance
in the organisation of the Symposium, and Mr. D.G. Moir, Secretary of the R.S.G.S.,
for help and support during the preparation for the Symposium.   Thanks are also due
to Mr. P.G. Adamson, Mr. C.B. Bremner, Mrs. G. Gowans, Mr. R. Harris and Mr. G.
Sanderman for help with the illustrations, and to Mrs. M. Robertson for typing the
manuscript.   The editors and publishers also thank the Department of Agriculture
and Fisheries for Scotland (Fig. 1.1), and the Scottish Development Department
(Fig. 8.1) for permission to publish copyright material.

CHAPTER 1

THE CONCEPT OF LAND QUALITY : AN OVERVIEW

J.T. Coppock

University of Edinburgh

ABSTRACT

Since 1939 there has been a growing demand for information about land including its
capability for other uses, largely because of pressures on rural land but also for
areas of falling populations and underused resources.   These demands have grown
piecemeal and a variety of bases has been used, mostly for subjective assessments.
The purposes have also varied, though most have been intended as aids to planning
and the aim is not always explicit.   No attempts to compare different assessments
have been published.   Computer-based systems offer the prospect of greater flexibility and of storing data in disaggregated form;   they also permit man-made characteristics to be incorporated as separate coverages.   Such coverages are costly and
ad hoc surveys may be more cost effective;   probably both comprehensive and local
surveys are required.   Such assessments should also be comprehendable by laymen.

KEYWORDS

ad hoc surveys;   agricultural assessments;   aids to planning;   purpose of assessment;
constituent components;   socio-economic parameters;   comprehensive appraisals.

INTRODUCTION

It has increasingly been accepted that the government of a modern state needs information on the characteristics and resources of the territory it controls and of the
population to which it is responsible.   National mapping and census taking are the
oldest of these functions and represent a continuing commitment to re-survey and the
taking of new censuses.   The Geological Survey was the first agency to be established to record resources in a systematic way, but there has been a growing demand
since 1939 for information on other resources, including the land itself.   Moreover, it is not merely information about the land that is required but also assessments of its quality, or more specifically, its suitability for a particular use,
since there can be no meaningful assessment of land quality overall.   Much of this
demand has arisen because of numerous pressures on rural land in the lowlands,
particularly from urban expansion, and a perceived need to conserve the best
resources, notably of agricultural land;   but information has also been needed in
areas of declining populations on the suitability of land for other potential uses,
such as forestry and recreation, and in response to a growing acceptance of conservation of both amenity and wildlife as an important area of public policy.

I

These perceptions of need have grown piecemeal, depending on the pressures for change, the political strength of vested interests, changing views about conservation and development, political goals and philosophies, and accidents of personalities and events.   Canada appears to be the only country to have attempted systematic assessments of its land, or more strictly, of its settled areas (which are themselves more than thirty times as large as Scotland) from a variety of viewpoints; the Canada Land Inventory comprises four coverages of land capability for agriculture, forestry, recreation and wildlife.   In Scotland the emphasis has been on assessments of farmland, and then primarily for its agricultural significance in the context of urban growth, though there has more recently been increasing attention to forestry, scenery and wildlife.

The assessment of agricultural land in Scotland had its origins in 1943, in an initiative of the Planning Division of the Department of Health.   As a result, officers of the Department of Agriculture began to map the lowlands at a scale of 1:10,560 on a seven-fold scheme that indicated the land's overall agricultural quality.   Although the resulting maps have never been published, they have been widely consulted and were used as a basis for the northern sheet of the land classification map of Great Britain, prepared by the Land Utilisation Survey and published in 1945 at a scale of 1:625,000.   This was the first, and until 1976, the only published map of land classification for the whole of Scotland; in that year, a map at a scale of 1:2,500,000 was included in the Scottish Development Department's Land Use Summary Sheet No. 1 (Fig. 1.1).   Surveys of suitability of land for forestry have been prepared for different parts of the country and a similar small-scale map was published in 1976 in Land Use Summary Sheet No. 2, showing land suitable for planting, though this land was not differentiated in any way according to degrees of suitability. Interest in the scenic quality of land goes back at least to the Addison Committee (1931) and several attempts have been made to produce maps of scenic value, notably by Linton (1968), and the Countryside Commission for Scotland's map of Scotland's Scenic Heritage (1978) in effect portrays the top category of such an assessment. Other evaluations of land quality have been made for parts of the country for a variety of purposes by both individual researchers and public bodies, such as the maps of Areas of Great Landscape value prepared by local authorities in Scotland (Coppock, 1968).

THE BASES AND PURPOSES OF ASSESSMENT

Many of these maps are first approximations, and this is also largely true of the classifications of the Canada Land Inventory.   A variety of bases has been used, though most are derived from subjective assessments, from soil maps and from topography.   In part these characteristics are due to the need for rapid coverage and to the fact that soil maps were not available for the whole country.   Whether, as Mackney (1962) has claimed, soil is *the* factor in land classification is a matter of debate, but many of the boundaries in any classification of rural land are likely to be physiographic features.   Since it may be necessary to compare assessments of land for different purposes and since independent surveys may well show small differences in the boundaries drawn that are not intended and do not express real differences on the ground, it can be argued that all assessments should be based upon physiographic units, though in any given assessment some units would be sub-divided and some amalgamated.   Such an approach has, of course, been attempted in various schemes of classification of terrain (e.g., Webster and Beckett, 1970) and forms an important part of the system of land evaluation adopted in Australia by the Division of Land Use Research in the Commonwealth Scientific and Industrial Research Organisation (Christian and Stewart, 1953).

The various schemes also differ widely in the purposes for which they have been made;

for land quality has meaning only in respect of a particular objective.   Most are
intended as aids to planning, whether to minimise the harm of transfers from existing
uses or to ensure that the range of alternatives for new uses is considered on its
merits.   The purpose for which a land classification is made is not always clearly
stated and assessments may sometimes be modified by policy restraints.   For example,
the land capability maps prepared by the Soil Survey of Scotland record seven categories of land, but whereas the top three refer only to agriculture, the remaining
four also make reference to suitability for recreation and forestry.   This is not
because the first three categories are unsuitable for either of these uses, but rather
because it is policy that the use of such land for non-agricultural purposes should
be discouraged.   It would be equally eroneous to assume that all the land shown as
suitable for forestry on Summary Sheet No. 2 was of equal quality for this purpose.
In the Canada Land Inventory, all land is graded according to its suitability for
each use, so that a given parcel could thus be rated highly for both farming and
forestry and any policy restraints could be applied later.   This difference in approach may be due partly to the fact that the Inventory was conceived as an aid to
rural development in marginal areas and was envisaged from the start as a computer-
based system, with the capability of overlying one or more assessments.   There have
been no published attempts to compare assessments of land quality for different purposes in Scotland, though this situation may change in the light of experience with
the pilot rural information system for the Kirkcaldy District; the TRIP data bank,
managed by the Planning Data Management Service (1979), has such a capability, if
only for grid squares.

CHARACTERISTICS OF ASSESSMENTS

In any consideration of what has been attempted in developing methods of assessing
land capability in Scotland, it is essential to bear in mind both what is desirable
in such systems and, equally important, what cannot be achieved.   It is not possible
to have an assessment that is universal, in the sense that it provides indications
of suitability for a wide range of uses, though (as noted earlier) some systems may
appear to incorporate more than one use.   Different assessments will be required
for different purposes, and it is only when the objectives are clearly defined that
a satisfactory assessment of land capability can be devised.   Even in respect of
land for agriculture, a system designed to indicate broad suitability for farming
in the context of planning decisions about urban expansion can give little guidance
on suitability for, say, horticultural crops; indeed, it would be possible to have
a whole family of agricultural assessments for each of the farming enterprises.

Nor can any system of classification be permanent; it must be based upon present
physical conditions, present technology and present capital investment in such features as levees and drainage channels.   One has only to recall the changing evaluations of the English Fenland or of the Chalk downs of southern England to appreciate
this point.   The first is perhaps unusual in indicating the effects of both capital
and investment and rapid environmental change, for the Fenland, once a watery waste
and now containing much of the first class agricultural land in Great Britain as a
result of investment in drainage, is now under threat because of the progressive dis-
appearance of the peat through erosion and aeration.   In respect of the chalklands,
it is technical and economic change that has led to successive revaluations, with
peaks marked by prehistoric farming, the golden hoof of the folded sheep and modern
mechanised farming, with its high inputs of fertiliser, separated by troughs marking
the drainage of the lowlands and the adoption of the heavy mouldboard plough and the
low-input farming of the years of agricultural depression between 1879 and 1939.

Assessments of capability can thus be only relatively short term, but they should
also be objective, repeatable and practicable.   The first two aims are, of course,
closely related, in that an objective method is likely to produce the same results
irrespective of the observer; on the other hand, most systems do require the exercise

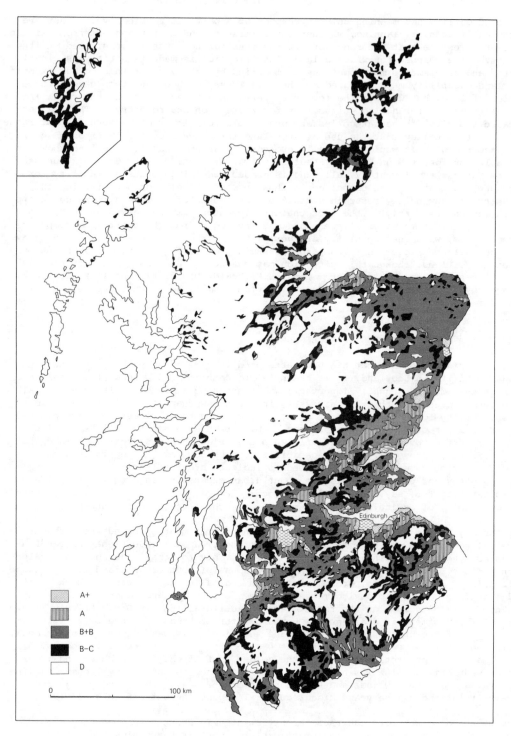

Fig. 1.1 Agricultural Land Classification

Source: Department of Agriculture and Fisheries for Scotland

FACTORS WHICH INFLUENCE CLASSIFICATION OF LAND IN SCOTLAND

A+   Category Land.   Factors Which Influence Classification

Highest quality land capable of growing all agricultural crops including intensive
market garden crops.   Deep well drained free loam, sandy loam, silt loam.   Level
or on a gentle slope with good reserves of moisture available.   Well supplied with
plant nutrients or is highly responsive to fertilisers.   No climatic factors restrict its agricultural use and yields are consistently high.

A   Category Land.   Factors Which Influence Classification

Good fertile land suitable for growing most crops but with some restrictions which
exclude it from A+ category.   Deep well drained loams and clays.   Level or on a
gentle slope with good reserves of moisture available.   Well supplied with plant
nutrients or is highly responsive to fertilisers.   No climatic factors seriously
restrict agricultural use to any major extent and yields are consistently high.

B+   Category Land.   Factors Which Influence Classification

Good land with more limited cropping potential.   Well drained loams, stoney and
sandy loams, clays.   Level to moderate slope.   Capable of growing good crops of
cereal, grass and roots but not so highly productive as Grade A.   Response to good
management.   Production suffers some restrictions resulting from soil texture, drainage or climatic conditions.

B   Category Land.   Factors Which Influence Classification

Medium land capable of growing average crops of grass, oats, barley and roots.   All
types of soil represented.   Slope may vary from level conditions to moderate steepness.   Capable of growing average crops for sale or home consumption under reasonable management.   Does not suffer from extremes of climatic conditions, soil structure, soil depth or stone content.

B-   Category Land.   Factors Which Influence Classification

The land of less good quality than medium, mostly given over to grass or for the
production of crops for stock feed.   Limited cropping potential due to adverse
climate, slope or soil characteristics including unsuitable texture, structure,
wetness, shallow depth, stoniness or low water holding capabilities.

C   Category Land.   Factors Which Influence Classification

Poor arable land only capable of restricted use, mostly in grass and only cultivated
to enable reseeding to take place.   Adverse soil characteristics include unsuitable
textures, structure, wetness, shallow depth, stoniness, low water holding capabilities.   Slope may vary from level to conditions of extreme steepness.   Inadequately
supplied with natural plant nutrients.   At higher elevations climatic conditions
tend to restrict growth and yields are low even when adequate manuring takes place.

D   Category Land.   Factors Which Influence Classification

Land of little agricultural value due to severe restrictions of soil, relief or climate or a combination of these.   Such land is generally under rough grazing or grass
except for the occasional pioneer forage crop.

of judgment, both in the choice of parameters for inclusion in the assessment and in the actual values or rankings to be attached to those parameters. What can be expected is that the bases of choice can be made explicit so that, as far as possible, another individual would come to the same conclusion on the same evidence and that, where appropriate, explicit rules will be formulated and quantitative measures adopted. The practicability of any method of assessment will also be governed by two related considerations, cost and time. There is not much point in devising elaborate systems that are expensive and demanding of skilled manpower. Changes in the use of land are occurring now and cannot usually be delayed for an ideal solution. Some compromise will generally be necessary between speed and comprehensiveness.

DISCUSSION TOPICS

In a review of methods of assessment issues that bear upon these considerations four topics merit discussion, viz., whether assessments should be stored as such or by their constituent components; whether man-made constraints should be incorporated in the assessments; whether nation-wide coverages are necessary; and how assessments of capability for different uses are to be compared. Since technical changes in the different land uses are likely to lead to some modification of the existing assessments, as they have done since the Second World War, separate storage in a computer-based system of data on the various components (soils, relief, drainage, climatic conditions and the like) would permit new assessments appropriate to the new technologies to be made quickly. Furthermore, not only could data be progressively replaced as better data became available but it would also be possible to establish statistical relationships between components and the classes that might have predictive value. Of course, this approach would require explicit rules about interpreting physical data and so exclude the kind of subjective assessments that have often been used in the past.

It has also been argued, notably by Hilton (1968) in relation to agricultural land quality, that account should be taken of man-made characteristics, such as size and layout of farms, since these can have the effect of either enhancing or diminishing the capability of the land. A record of such features could, of course, be included as a separate data set in a computer-based system and it may be noted that the Canada Land Inventory, though based on physical quality, does include coverages of present land use, climate and socio-economic parameters (though it does not maintain the components of the physical assessments in disaggregated form).

The third issue is a more pragmatic one. Making appraisal of land quality takes time, uses scarce resources of skilled manpower and costs money; yet the information is not required simultaneously over the whole country, and some may not be needed for a long time. Would it not be better to use scarce resources where and when they were required rather than attempt national coverages which, if they are to be useful, must be done quickly and be, to varying degrees, provisional? Arguments in favour of the first approach are that resources can be concentrated where they are needed, that it is at the large scale that actual decisions are made, and that there is no long-term commitment to a classification of land quality that may have to change. Against, it can be claimed that a national perspective is often necessary where major changes (or even cumulative minor changes) are concerned and that there may be insufficient time for detailed local surveys to be made (as with the siting of oil-related industries). Does the answer lie in some combination of the two approaches?

Lastly, it will increasingly be necessary to compare the results of one system of assessing land capability with those of another; and whilst their feasibility of doing so will in part depend on the accuracy of field observation and on the interpretation of boundaries between classes, it also depends on the existence of common topographic base map of high standard on which the different assessments can be recorded. This will be increasingly important in the future as computer-based information systems develop and include digital map records of both the topographic base on which the assessments are recorded and the assessments themselves (Royal Society, 1978). This will equally be the case where such information is derived from field survey or, as they will increasingly be (at least in part) from remote sensing. The criterion for evaluating the usefulness of such assessments will be their success in serving the purposes for which they were designed.

CONCLUSIONS

There can be little doubt that planners find it helpful to have such guidance, both in day-to-day decisions and in justifying proposals at public inquiries. It is accordingly helpful if schemes of classification can be comprehended by the laymen who may have to make the decisions; for both they and their professional advisers will need to be convinced of the soundness of the advice such schemes provide. If they are, it will be increasingly feasible, as computerised systems develop, to relate not only different kinds of assessment of capability but also capability and existing use or other categories of information, to monitor changes in land use against capabilities and to provide the inputs of information that are essential to more effective policy making.

REFERENCES

Bibby, J.S., (1973). Land capability, Ch. 5 in J. Tivy (Ed). *The Organic Resources of Scotland,* Oliver and Boyd, Edinburgh.

Christian, C.S. and G.A. Stewart, (1953). *General Report on Survey of Katherine-Darwin Region 1946.* Land Research Series No. 1, CSIRO, Canberra.

Coppock, J.T., (1968). The Countryside (Scotland) Act and the geographer. *Scot. Geogr. Mag.,* 84, 201-11.

Countryside Commission for Scotland, (1978). *Scotland's Scenic Heritage,* The Commission, Battleby.

Elgood, L.A., (Ed), (1961). *Natural Resources in Scotland,* Scottish Council (Development and Industry), Edinburgh.

Environment Canada, (1978). *The Canada Land Inventory, Objectives, Scope and Organisation,* The Department, Ottawa.

Hilton, N., (1968). Land classification, in *Studies in Applied Geography,* Special Publication No.1, Institute of British Geographers, London.

Linton, D.L., (1968). Scenery as a natural resource, *Scott. Geogr. Mag.,* 84, 219-38.

Mackney, D., (1962). Soil - the factor in land classification, in *The Classification of Agricultural Land in Britain,* Technical Report No. 8, Agricultural Land Service, HMSO, London.

Planning Data Management Service, (1979). *Service Description,* PDMS, Edinburgh.

Rees, W.E., (1977). *The Canada Land Inventory in Perspective,* Fisheries and Environment, Canada, Ottawa.

Royal Society, (1978). *The Future Role of the Ordnance Survey,* The Society, London.

Scottish Development Department, (1976-). *National Planning Series, Land Use Summary Sheets,* The Department, Edinburgh.

Stamp, L.D., (1950). The classification of land, Ch. 17, in *The Land of Britain : its Use and Misuse,* 2nd edn., Longmans, London.

Webster, R. and P.H.T. Beckett, (1970). Terrain classification and evaluation using air photography : a review of work at Oxford; *Photogrammetria,* 26, 51-75.

CHAPTER 2
THE ROLE OF REMOTE SENSING IN LAND ASSESSMENT

R.P. Kirby
University of Edinburgh

ABSTRACT

Remote sensing is one of the basic preliminaries to land assessment, of relevance in both the acquisition and analysis of information on terrain. It mostly fulfils an auxiliary role, combining with ground observations, but partial land assessments can sometimes be derived almost entirely by remote sensing methods. The imagery prin- cipally used in Scotland is conventional aerial photographs, but sensors using wave- lengths beyond the visible range are sometimes used experimentally. The availability of imagery of Scotland is described, particularly aerial photographs from military, civil and commercial sources, and Landsat satellite imagery. Three cases where remote sensing has been used as the principal method of investigation are described: the Scottish coastal survey of ecological habitats, the peat survey of the Scottish Soil Survey and experimental classification of terrain in the Western Highlands. Numerous other examples are presented where air photo interpretation has been used to acquire supplementary information.

Some natural limitations to remote sensing in Scotland are noted, together with sug- gestions as to how the repetitive small-scale coverage from Earth satellites might be used in the future to provide stringent monitoring of changes in land use and of environmental deterioration.

KEYWORDS

Auxiliary role of remote sensing; aerial photographs; satellite imagery; monitoring environmental change; coastal survey of ecological habitats; terrain classification.

INTRODUCTION

It is a happy coincidence that one of the first modern papers on the use of aerial photography for land assessment in Scotland was published in the Scottish Geographical Magazine, by the Society sponsoring this symposium. The paper, by Wyllie Fenton in 1951, describes the vegetation and agricultural activities shown on two single aerial photographs taken of adjacent areas at the north end of the Pentland Hills, Midlothian. The account is unstructured and incomplete, yet makes interesting and even novel read- ing because of the author's familiarity with the area on the ground. In the quarter- century or so since this short paper was written, and notably since the late 1960s, air photo interpretation has blossomed into the subject of remote sensing, with new

9

sensors to record what is on the ground, aided by developments in data handling and computer mapping. Remote sensing today is one of the basic preliminaries to land assessment (Mitchell, 1973). When land use data are required, no other method of acquisition or analysis is as efficient, and it is not surprising that remote sensing technology makes one of its biggest and most significant contributions in this field.

USES OF REMOTE SENSING IN LAND ASSESSMENT

Although it must be recognised that data acquired by remote sensing are only a surrogate for direct ground observations, they are often more immediately available, more economically gathered in terms of both time and labour costs, and may well yield a better result. A modicum of experience of the local terrain remains essential but often the expensive ground observations can be quite limited.

The simple role of aerial photographs for interpreting terrain features in their correct spatial relationships is well known, but there are in fact at least two different roles - the systematic analysis and integrating role for observers who know what they are looking for, and the contemplative role for observers, like Fenton in 1951, who possibly do not. This point has been made clearly by Goodier (1971) in a similar ecological context. In the second role of leisured browsing, it is easier with aerial photographs than with any other investigative technique to recognise and investigate fresh spatial relationships amongst the elements of the terrain. In land assessment, which combines so many cognitive and analytical skills, such preliminary contemplation of a miniaturised three-dimensional model of the landscape is usually well worthwhile.

The standard requirements in assessing any aspect of terrain are to determine, firstly, the present distributions, secondly, the inter-relationships between the distributions and, thirdly, to consider the changes in time. In determining the status quo, it is sometimes necessary to begin with the fundamental physiographical characteristics of geology and topography. These are essentially unchanging, and in Scotland remote sensing has only a residual part left to play in determining these characteristics because of the quality and coverage now achieved by maps published by the Ordnance Survey and the Institute of Geological Sciences. The other unchanging element, the soil, may be regarded as the fundamental factor of any land assessment, but cannot be recognised and classified directly by means of remote sensing in Scotland as the soil is concealed from sight by the continuous vegetation cover. Soil types may, however, be inferred from a consideration of topography, geology, vegetation and drainage together.

Remote sensing is much more suited to describing the distributions of, and changes in, natural vegetation, land use and agricultural resources. The characteristic differences on aerial photographs of the surface reflectances of plants as well as differences in texture and shape allow fairly easy discrimination and hence classification into land-cover types. Moreover, because of the dynamic character of the rural landscape, there is great scope for the use of multidate or sequential remote sensing imagery to build up a pattern of change. Such changes may have different causes: they may be purely cyclical, as with phenological change in permanent vegetation, indicated by senescence and shedding of leaves. Alternatively, the changes may indicate natural but non-seasonal developments, such as increase in the height of trees, the areal spread of bracken or heather, and vegetation stress, whether this is due to drought, to disease or to insect pests. Changes in agricultural land most obviously reflect the patterns of cropping, either by annual field crops or the longer periods of cropping in forestry. This dynamic aspect is of vital concern, whether the information is used directly in land management, or is considered broadly as part of the planning process.

CHOICE AND AVAILABILITY OF REMOTE SENSING IMAGERY IN SCOTLAND

Far more investigations use existing aerial photographs than commission new photography; existing aerial photographs are readily available and prints are inexpen-
sive.   However, as the photographs were not taken with the user's specific interest
in mind, they will normally serve only as a general-purpose familiarisation with the
scene.   The coverage of black and white aerial photographs for Scotland is shown in
Figs. 2.1-2.3.   In each case the coverage shown is for standard panchromatic vertical photography of recent date, the distinction between the figures being on the basis
of photographic scale.   About half of Scotland is covered by the largest group of
scales (Fig. 2.1), particularly within the Central Lowlands, the Northeast, and coastal areas generally, but much of this coverage is achieved from many overlapping small
schemes that can still result in small unphotographed blocks occurring anywhere.
The main highland and upland areas of Scotland are covered by modern imagery only at
medium and smaller scales (Figs. 2.2 and 2.3), much of the photography forming the
basis of the Ordnance Survey's programme of remapping at the 1:10,000 scale.   The
coverages for the Highlands and Southern Uplands in Figs. 2.2 and 2.3 are largely
complementary.

The coverage of natural colour and colour infrared photography for the post 1969 period in Scotland is much more limited (Fig. 2.4).   Much of the Central Lowlands and
a large proportion of the Scottish coastline have been covered by natural colour
photography at various scales, and colour infrared photography exists for several
blocks in the Central Lowlands as well as for the Cromarty Firth.   Elsewhere the
absence of any colour photography emphasises the greater cost and difficulty of acquiring this sort of imagery.

The Scottish library of modern air photographs as well as of much pre-1969 material
is housed by the Scottish Development Department (SDD) in Edinburgh.   Facilities
for browsing and purchasing are provided for standard aerial photographs taken by
the Royal Air Force (RAF), the Ordnance Survey and the British commercial air survey companies.   In addition, browse facilities exist for Landsat satellite multi-
spectral (MSS) imagery, although this is ordered through the United Kingdom national
point of contact with Earthnet, the Royal Aircraft Establishment, Farnborough.

Where existing photography is inadequate in respect of scale, resolution, or type of
film, or is too old, then new imagery must be commissioned.   Obtaining the best
images that are reasonably practicable should involve the user in very careful planning.   The objectives of the scheme must be clearly thought through and defined, and
then translated into the appropriate photographic specifications, for example, time
of year, time of day, state of tide (if coastal), film, filter and scale.   The best
images can be obtained only if care and attention are given to these factors, and
this is particularly true in land assessment studies that involve discrimination of
vegetation.   It is unfortunately too often the case that the customer, in his sat-
isfaction at being able to commission new photography at all, does not give precise
instructions and is provided with standard panchromatic or natural colour prints at
a nominal scale.   These may be less costly but will probably also be of less use
than prints produced to an exact specification.

If rigorous interpretation is to be attempted, it is highly desirable that in addition to careful planning, ground truth observations, which are almost always necessary anyway, should be made at the same time as the photography is taken.   This requirement involves further co-operation between customer and supplier of the photographs.

Vertical aerial photographs of guaranteed high quality can be commissioned to customer's specifications from the constituent firms of the British Air Survey Association (BKS, Fairey Surveys, Hunting Surveys, Meridian) which have the aircraft and
expensive equipment to provide the aerial photographs and produce photogrammetric

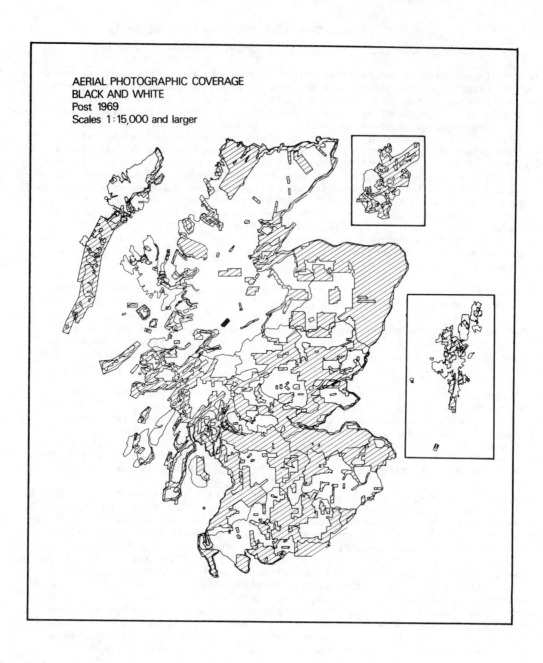

AERIAL PHOTOGRAPHIC COVERAGE
BLACK AND WHITE
Post 1969
Scales 1:15,000 and larger

Fig. 2.1 Aerial Photographic Coverage (black and white),
Scales 1:15,000 and Larger

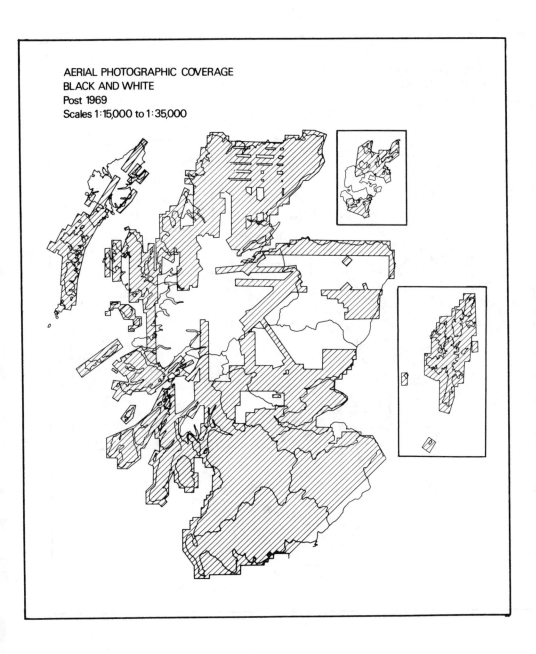

AERIAL PHOTOGRAPHIC COVERAGE
BLACK AND WHITE
Post 1969
Scales 1:15,000 to 1:35,000

Fig. 2.2 Aerial Photographic Coverage (black and white),
Scales 1:15,000 to 1:35,000

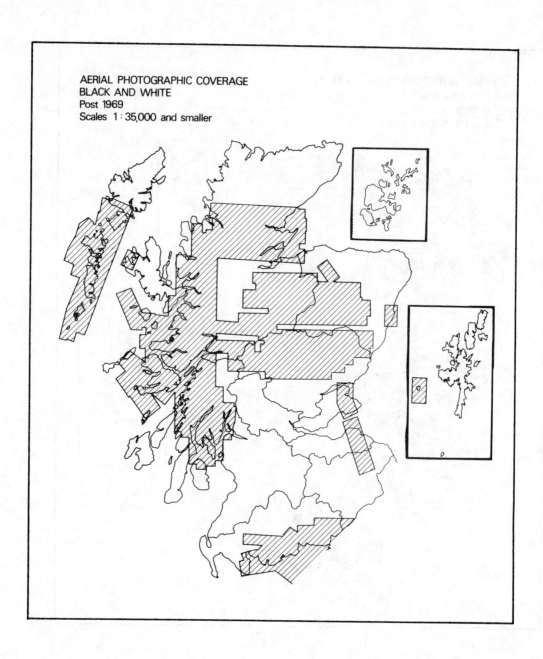

AERIAL PHOTOGRAPHIC COVERAGE
BLACK AND WHITE
Post 1969
Scales 1:35,000 and smaller

Fig. 2.3 Aerial Photographic Coverage (black and white),
Scales 1:35,000 and Smaller

plots from them.   Photo interpretation and resource surveys will also be conducted
if required, but the lesser amounts of equipment and the different sorts of expertise
necessary to do this mean that the customer may well choose to work with the imagery
himself.

In addition, smaller aerial photographic firms, for example, John Dower Studios in
Edinburgh, are available to take oblique aerial photographs of use in reconnaissance
and promotional exercises.   A fine selection of Scottish oblique aerial photographs
is provided by Glen and Williams (1972).   The user may also prefer to obtain his
own reconnaissance imagery, using small format 35 mm or 70 mm cameras from either a
light aircraft (for example, Moreno, 1970; Stove, 1978) or a captive balloon (for
example, Duffield and Forsyth, 1972).   With such facilities, costs are minimised
but the results are suitable only for general appraisal.   It is not possible to
obtain metric photography for photogrammetric mapping by these crude methods, but
there is some possibility of their use in graphical revison of maps, provided that
there are sufficient map control points.

Between the high-quality verticals supplied by commercial companies and the low-
quality obliques, there is an obvious gap in supply.   Particularly in studies of
land assessment, cheaper small-format imagery with the exact photographic characteristics would be more useful than more expensive full-format verticals with the emphasis on photogrammetric requirements, and the commercial companies have been slow to
fill this gap.   To satisfy their specialist needs, the Forestry Commission employs
its own pilot-photographer to take oblique low altitude photographs throughout the
United Kingdom.   The Cambridge University Committee for Aerial Photography does
likewise for archaeology and general rural environmental studies.

APPLICATIONS IN SCOTTISH LAND ASSESSMENT

Accepting that land assessment, even if limited to rural land use, is a broad topic
covering both the acquisition and the evaluation of land capability, then remote
sensing, as one of the basic constituent techniques, can be used in a range of ways.
It is uncommon in Scotland, as in the rest of the United Kingdom, for remote sensing
to be the principal method in land assessment.   This is largely for reasons related
to the historical dominance of the Ordnance Survey's national series of topographical
maps and plans; remote sensing mostly fulfils an auxiliary role alongside map and
census studies.

Conventional aerial photographs overwhelmingly predominate in the list of types of
imagery used, and are likely to continue to do so.   Other airborne sensors have
been used experimentally, for example, multispectral photography using a Vinten 70
mm camera system for South Harris and Gairloch (Greenwood, 1974), and thermal surveys of coal bings and coastal waters in the Lothians by Fairey Surveys in 1972,
using an EMI thermal linescan unit.   But such methods have not been widely used
outside the urban and industrial environment.   The examples given below are of published articles, most of which have used specially-commissioned aerial photographs.
These examples may not properly represent the correct balance of users in studies
of land assessment, but merely some of the principal users.   As the visitors' book
for those using the browse facilities in the SDD air photo library shows, many of
these are from universities, government planning and research departments, government-
financed organisations such as the Nature Conservancy Council, and from industry,
whose air photo researches do not generate publications directly.   In addition,
a large case study being carried out for the Scottish Office in the Cromarty Firth
area with reference to oil-related industries and land use and involving specially-
commissioned sequential aerial photography is referred to in the final section.

Although there are no Scottish examples of remote sensing producing a full land
assessment, unlike England and Wales (Genderen and Smith, 1976) or continental

Europe (Haefner, 1967), there are several examples where remote sensing has acted as a primary data source or basis for analysis, and hence has contributed to the assessment of some elements of the landscape. The survey of Scottish coastal habitats (Kirby, 1977, 1978) is a case in point, and is the only country-wide example. This survey mainly involved the acquisition of data together with some limited analysis of stored data. Commissioned by the Nature Conservancy Council, the survey has attempted to provide the basic information for answering the specific enquiries of planners and scientists. Data relating to many aspects of the coastal ecological habitats were collected from conventional natural colour and black and white aerial photographs. About 300,000 items of data relating to nearly 2000 one-kilometre squares of the National Grid were stored in a computer bank for which facilities for search, classification and analysis are provided using the TRIP package to give tabular and graphical output. The coastal classification was predetermined and the data gathered objectively, the whole survey stopping short of the stage of assessment where subjective judgments are frequently called for.

In contrast, the study of land evaluation using air photo interpretation undertaken for the sample area of Kintyre jointly by soil scientists from Oxford University and from the Macaulay Institute for Soil Research (Lawrance and others, 1977) aims at achieving a simple hierarchical classification procedure directly. Classification of terrain into land systems and land facets is attempted on the same basis as some of the authors have used successfully elsewhere (Webster and Beckett, 1970), with the essential objective of providing the basis for acquiring information on soil and on land capability which is of practical use to the local planner, agricultural adviser or road engineer. The land facet is the basic unit of the classification, being defined as a unit uniformly manageable under moderately-intensive land use. It is also recognisable on aerial photographs. The results of the Scottish sample study, although giving some encouragement to the idea of a full land classification from aerial photographs, are poorer than from ground observations. Furthermore, it was found difficult to map soil complexes from their appearance on the aerial photographs without local ground experience, although patterned facets can be mapped from photographs.

An attempt is also being made from the Macaulay Institute for Soil Research to assess the economic resource of peat in Scotland and, by extension, the land value of the peat-covered areas (Stove, 1978). In this work a large range of modern remote sensing imagery and photogrammetric equipment is used, including comparison between simultaneous Landsat and aerial photographic material; but the study is still in an experimental stage.

Scotland is deficient in a modern national map of land cover types, the best currently available still being the reconnaissance survey of natural vegetation by Geddes and Stamp at the 1:625,000 scale, published in 1953. The deficiency is most serious for non-arable land, where agricultural census data provide no further breakdown of rough grazing. Vegetation and geomorphology maps have however been produced by photogrammetry and air photo interpretation for a number of special areas, of which notable examples are the Sands of Forvie National Nature Reserve at a scale of 1:7,500 (Wright and Ritchie, 1975) and the Island of Rhum at the 1:20,000 scale (Williams, 1971). In both cases the photogrammetric plotting was carried out at the University of Glasgow. For the 400 km² of the Gairloch conservation unit in Wester Ross, a provisional vegetation map with fourteen types of vegetation was produced by interpretation of existing panchromatic aerial photographs (Goldsmith, 1972) Remote sensing has also been used at Gairloch for assessments of wildlife conservation under controlled conditions (Nichol, 1977).

While the rural landscape, and especially agricultural land, is responsive to study by techniques of remote sensing, the urban landscape is both more complicated and more detailed, making the extraction of data on urban land use much more difficult. In urban studies, planners and geographers consequently use aerial photographs mainly for browsing and have not placed much emphasis on imagery as a primary source of thematic data.   For example, the planners concerned with Stonehouse New Town (Clark, 1974) expressed enthusiasm about the orthomosaic and the colour infrared prints available, but did not appear to be using either to provide fundamentally new information.   Rural settlements are simpler in form and function and so respond more readily to techniques of remote sensing.   The role of aerial photography in archaeological discovery of early rural settlements and abandoned isolated features is too well known to require any general comment.   The presence of archaeological features may occasionally lead to local planning constraints and so alter the effective land capability, but archaeological features alone generally have little weight in planning matters in comparison with the economic aspects of land use. For example, although the site of the Torness nuclear power station on the East Lothian coastline includes important archaeological monuments, colour aerial photographs taken in 1974 have revealed 16 previously unrecognised ancient monuments along a 4 km coastal strip between Thorntonloch and Barns Ness (Maxwell, 1975), and some of these cannot now be recovered because of disturbance of the site.

Also in southeast Scotland, Parry (1973, 1976) has used aerial photographs as a secondary source to register the probable sites of former farm settlements in moorland areas.   He found in this historical study that interpretation was better served by the repeat coverages of RAF photography taken in spring and autumn than by the once-off coverage of higher quality Ordnance Survey photography, even though the RAF photography was of inferior resolution, scale and metric qualities.

Current rural population densities are difficult to determine from remotely sensed imagery but may be estimated indirectly by comparison with current land use, which is easily established by remote sensing.   Morrison (1978) has attempted to determine experimentally the nature of the relationship between rural population density and land use for the Scottish Highlands by comparing land-use distributions derived from Landsat data with data from the population census available for kilometre squares, but the method appears to be more workable at present in underdeveloped countries with extensive rather than intensive land-use patterns.   When the human element is involved in any land assessment, inter-relationships are difficult to express in quantitative terms, although they are often intuitively apparent.   For instance, the broad relationship between afforestation and population structure in parts of rural Scotland is well known, as the forestry industry requires forestry workers who produce permanent if localised, social structures.   Darling, writing in 1955 on the social situation of the crofting townships, perceptively noted that various sorts of social malaise are much more prevalent in rural districts where forest cover has been removed than in those where forest cover had been preserved.   Whereas social structure is too intangible to yield directly to such a frontal attack as air photo interpretation, remote sensing can provide data on the distribution of trees and so provide a lead.

SCOTTISH PROSPECTS AND DIFFICULTIES

Assessors of land quality must have comprehensive and current information if they are to have any hope of promoting orderly use of the land.   Although remote sensing provides only one of the many kinds of information available to them, its archival value and the possibilities it offers of seeing frequent and up-to-date imagery should be strong attractions.   Nevertheless, for a number of reasons, remote sensing has not been used as much in Scotland for land assessment as in some other technically-advanced countries.   The first reason may simply be that the need does not arise to the same extent as elsewhere, because of the efficiency of alternative systems of ground-based data gathering.   However, a survey in England and Wales that has not so far been repeated for Scotland involved the commissioning in 1975 by the Secretary of State for the Environment of a project to map all the so-called developed areas, that is, areas of continuous urban development, by means of remote sensing.   This survey of developed land was produced by interpretation of photographs taken in 1969 by the RAF at 1:60,000 scale which were plotted onto overlays fitting the 1:50,000 map series of the Ordnance Survey.   The survey, which was completed within twelve months, has resulted in the compilation of a series of 124 land-use maps of the whole of England and Wales which will be used, together with the statictical data derived from them, to form an important base line against which to monitor subsequent changes in the nature, extent, and distribution of the urbanised areas (Genderen and Smith, 1976).   In Scotland, no such national series of land use maps has been prepared, the assessment and monitoring of land use being controlled by different agencies than in England and Wales.

As a preliminary step in the further testing of remote sensing for environmental monitoring in Scotland, in 1977 the Central Research Unit of the Scottish Development Department invited an independent aerial survey company to carry out a comprehensive research project using the Cromarty Firth as a test area.   Aerial photographs in colour and colour infrared were specially commissioned for this project (Fig. 2.4). The objectives of the study (Fairey Surveys Scotland Ltd., 1978) were to assess the usefulness of remote sensing generally, compared with other methods of environmental sensing, and to assess the value of remote sensing specifically for monitoring environmental pollution in the Cromarty Firth.   A series of nine detailed case studies was selected, including classification and changes in agricultural crops, land use, coastal vegetation and landforms, coniferous trees, quarrying and sources of effluent

The level of interpretation adopted throughout the case studies was everywhere very low, mostly a simple identification and description of ground features.   Even this identification was not always successful, as in the case of agricultural crop types. Nothing was attempted by way of systematic analysis in land classification, statistical assessment, or any form of mensuration, so that the specific conclusions on the Cromarty Firth test area represent a very simplified version of what could have been obtained considering the high quality sequential imagery and ground information available.   Furthermore, the assessment of the general usefulness of remote sensing compared with other methods is not valid, as the interpretations have not been taken to their reasonable limits.   As such, the interpretations are far from persuasive on the true potential of remote sensing compared with ground-based methods of land assessment.

In mitigation of this low non-technical level of interpretation it must be pointed out that a further objective of the research project was to familiarise staff of the Scottish Development Department with all aspects of environmental monitoring, so that the entire project was also a training exercise.   If it was necessary to hold the level of interpretation as low as this on educational grounds, then the different objectives of the project were probably incompatible.   Also a second reason why remote sensing has not been used much in Scotland for land assessment suggests itself.   This is the limited technical capacity of the central planning authorities to work with remote sensing imagery, possibly because of previous neglect of the existing specialist training facilities provided by universities and commercial companies in this fast-developing field.

A third, less controversial, reason is the physical difficulty of obtaining imagery at the visible wavelengths over Scotland compared with other countries.   This is due to the combination of latitude and maritime climate which produce conditions unsuited to aerial photography for all but the better days of the summer months. The poor weather during the summer of 1978, for example, meant that very few days were available for aerial photography, with one commercial company that operates in Scotland fulfilling only 15 per cent of the planned output at best quality colour and colour infrared photography.   Cloud cover has similarly restricted the availability of good quality Landsat multispectral scanner (MSS) and return beam vidicon (RBV) imagery, notwithstanding the 18-day frequency with which the satellites pass over each part of Scotland.   During 1978, very little cloud-free Landsat imagery

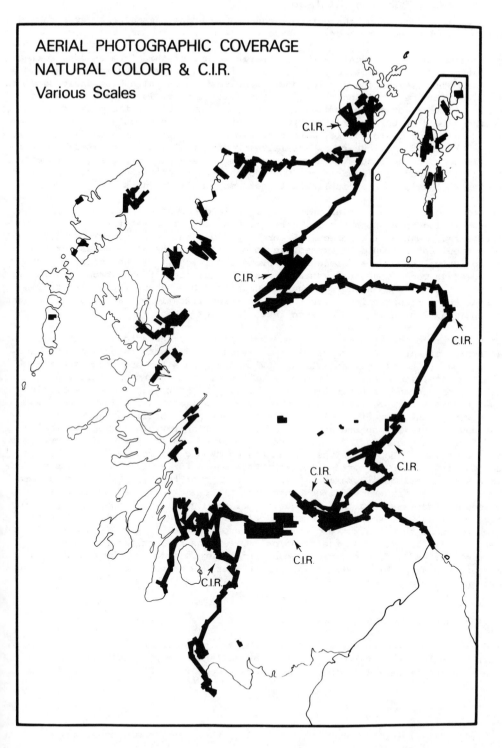

AERIAL PHOTOGRAPHIC COVERAGE
NATURAL COLOUR & C.I.R.
Various Scales

Fig. 2.4 Aerial Photographic Coverage, Natural Colour and
Colour Infrared

was acquired of any parts of the United Kingdom as numerous passes were never recorded and climatic conditions were poor for those that were.

A fourth reason is to be sought in the escalating costs of this form of data collection, together with the relatively low level of funding of projects involving remote sensing for both research and development. The cost of aerial photographic services in the United Kingdom is rising steeply. Satellite imagery is currently provided at a nominal charge but there is clearly a move, recognisable in the political lobbies in the United States, towards putting the satellite sensing on a more commercial basis. Such a move could quickly make nonsense of any cost-benefit studies, and it would be realistic for all users of satellite or of aerial imagery to assume higher costs of imagery in the future. However, if remote sensing can prove itself further by successful use and particularly by knowledgeable representations at both research and managerial level, then it is likely to gain more influential support.

The future of conventional aerial photography in land assessment would appear to be that of continuing in a support role, especially at larger scales for customer-orientated projects. National coverages of aerial photographs at regular intervals have been advocated, but it would be impossible to obtain these on given dates for Scotland both on logistical grounds and because of cloud conditions. In any case, repeated general coverage could give only general perspectives, useful for a broad desciptive survey such as is used in Sweden in the Economic Land Use national photomap series, but without the correct scale or other technical specifications that should be sought in most individual planning or research investigations.

Repetitive coverage for speculative purposes is of course the strong advantage of the Landsat series of earth resource satellites, which are designed to provide MSS data in digital and graphical form as well as RBV camera scenes for one broad spectral band. Such satellite data offer the possibility for the future of monitoring changes in visible land use and of environmental quality. Landsat images offer something to almost everyone for browsing, largely because each image covers 34,000 km^2, but, beyond browsing, the current level of ground resolution is still too gross for adequate ground discrimination and analysis of the Scottish terrain, given the small sizes of field and their varied use. The impressive results of the Large Area Crop Inventory Experiment (LACIE) in the United States should not lead us to suppose that a sequential inspection of terrain in, say, Strathmore for monitoring biomass production is equally possible at present. On the assumption that the Landsat programme continues beyond its experimental/developmental stages so that the quantity of satellite imagery increases and that the quality of resolution also continues to improve, technical problems will remain in decoding, classifying and analysing the data. Such problems mean that Landsat digital data cannot be used in a quick-browse capacity. But even if it is assumed that the technical operations for monitoring changes in land uses can be reduced to a rapid standard procedure carried out by a central authority, organisational problems will still remain over how to make decisions fast enough for worthwhile action to be taken.

ACKNOWLEDGMENT

The kind assistance is acknowledged of Mr. A.W. Brotchie, the Air Photographs Officer at Scottish Development Department, in making available the original drawings from which the figures on aerial photographic coverage were derived.

REFERENCES

Clark,W.A.S., (1974). Orthophotography applied to the planning of Stonehouse New Town. *Photogrammetric Record* 8, No. 44, 154-166.
Darling, F. Fraser, (1955). *West Highland Survey*. Oxford Univ. Press, Oxford.

Duffield, B.S. and J.F. Forsyth, (1972). Assessing the impacts of recreation use on coastal sites in East Lothian. *The Use of Aerial Photography in Countryside Research*. Countryside Commission Pub. 54, 37-45, The Commission, London.

Fairey Surveys Scotland Ltd. (1978). *Final Report for the Cromarty Firth project area*. Report submitted to Scottish Development Department, Edinburgh.

Fenton, E.W., (1951). Vegetation and agricultural activities as shown by aerial photographs. *Scot. Geogr. Mag.* 67, 105-109.

Genderen, J.L. van and T.F. Smith, (1976). A national land use survey of the developed areas of England and Wales by remote sensing. *Proc. 10th International Sympos. on Remote Sensing of the Environment*. Ann Arbor, 383-392.

Glen, A. and M. Williams, (1972). *Scotland from the Air*. Heinemann, London.

Goldsmith, F.B., (1972). Vegetation mapping in upland areas and the development of conservation management plans. *The Use of Aerial Photography in Countryside Research*. Countryside Commission Pub. 54, 18-24. The Commission, London.

Goodier, R., (1971). Aerial photography and the ecologist. *The Application of Aerial Photography to the Work of the Nature Conservancy*. Nature Conservancy, Edinburgh, 1-5.

Greenwood, J.G.W. (Ed)., (1974). *Remote Sensing Evaluation Flights, 1971. Part II, South Harris and Gairloch Area*. Natural Environment Research Council, Pub. Series C, No. 12, The Council, London.

Haefner, H., (1967). Airphoto interpretation of rural land use in Western Europe. *Photogrammetria* 22, 143-152.

Kirby, R.P., (1977). *Remote Sensing of Scottish Coastal Habitats*. TRRU Research Report 34, Dept. of Geography, University of Edinburgh.

Kirby, R.P., (1979). Some organisational problems of a remote sensing inventory based on the National Grid. *Proc. 5th Ann. Conf. of Remote Sensing Society*. Durham, 1978.

Lawrance, C.J. and others, (1977). The use of air photo interpretation for land evaluation in the western Highlands of Scotland. *Catena* 4, 341-357.

Maxwell, G., (1975). New archaeological prospects. *Fairey Surveys Newsletter* 15.

Mitchell, C.W., (1973). *Terrain evaluation*. Longmans, London.

Moreno, R., (1970). *The value of 35 mm Vertical Aerial Photography for Forest Surveys*. Unpub. Ph.D. thesis, University of Edinburgh.

Morrison, A., (1979). A comparison of Landsat and census data in the Scottish Highlands. *Proc. 5th Ann. Conf. of Remote Sensing Society*, Durham, 1978.

Nichol, J.E., (1977). Collection and processing of remote sensing data related to wildlife conservation in natural environments. *Proc. 10th International Sympos. on Remote Sensing of the Environment*, Ann Arbor, 369-372.

Parry, M.L., (1973). *Changes in the Upper Limit of Cultivation in Southeast Scotland 1600-1900*. Unpub. Ph.D. thesis, University of Edinburgh.

Parry, M.L., (1976). The abandonment of upland settlement in southern Scotland. *Scot. Geogr. Mag.* 92, 50-60.

Stove, G.C., (1978). The development of remote sensing methods and an automated photogrammetric-cartographic system for peat resource surveys in Scotland. *Proc. 5th Ann. Conf. of Remote Sensing Society*, Durham, 1978.

Webster, R. and P.H.T. Beckett, (1970). Terrain classification and evaluation using air photography : a review of recent work at Oxford. *Photogrammetria* 26, 51-75.

Williams, H.J., (1971). The use of aerial photography in general resources and land use survey. *The Application of Aerial Photography to the Work of the Nature Conservancy*. Nature Conservancy, Edinburgh, 6-20.

Wright, R. and W. Ritchie, (1975). *The survey and photo-interpretation of the Sands of Forvie, Aberdeenshire*. Odell Memorial Monograph, No.4, Dept. of Geography, University of Aberdeen.

DISCUSSION

Comment by R. Goodier, Nature Conservancy Council, Edinburgh.

I think most people would agree that the use of remote sensing for land assessment in Britain has undergone a relatively slow development. Some of the reasons for this have been identified by Dr. Kirby in his paper, not least of which is the historical dominance of the Ordnance Survey national series of maps and plans. A sizeable proportion of British practitioners of the application of remote sensing to land assessment have learned their art or trade abroad in lands, not necessary technologically advanced, where the absence of good maps made the use of aerial photographs imperative.

Dr. Kirby laid emphasis, rightly I think, on the key role that remote sensing has to play in relation to assessing the distribution and changes in such major land attributes as natural vegetation, land use and agricultural resources - *natural* vegetation in this context presumably meaning vegetation comprising mainly or entirely native species rather than the rather small amount that has not been substantially influenced by man's actions.

I am glad that Dr. Kirby gave prominence to the unique facility provided by the Scottish Development Department's library of air photography. I know that the Nature Conservancy Council greatly value it and have made substantially increased use of its resources during the past three or four years. I would be interested to know if this increased utilisation in recent years has been a general feature.

I was interested in the mention made by Dr. Kirby of the use of aerial photographs obtained to less exacting standards than those needed for photogrammetry. We have, I think, sometimes been over-apologetic for making do with something less than the best - but the reference to Parry's work indicates that material of the highest technical quality may not always be the most useful for the job in hand. If one can be sensibly opportunistic one can often get what is needed at surprisingly low cost.

Dr. Kirby mentioned the NCC sponsored survey of Scottish Coastal Habitats carried out by his department. The details of the project itself have been described in the report published by TRRU, and in Dr. Kirby's paper at the Durham Symposium last year. The results represent a very interesting body of information but I'm sorry to have to admit that we in the NCC have been slower than we would have liked in making full use of it and we have only now reached the stage where we are beginning to explore its use for analytical and management purposes. One of the reasons for this has been the work required to translate something originally undertaken as a research project into a management tool readily accessible for day to day use.

Dr. Kirby has mentioned the lack of a modern national map of land cover types, nothing comprehensive having been produced since that published by Geddes and Stamp in 1953. Perhaps the work described by Dr. Bibby in the previous paper will go some way towards providing this for although there is no immediate intention to produce a vegetation map *per se*, I understand that the vegetation or vegetation complex characteristics of each of the soil categories mapped will be included in the key to the maps and described in the accompanying monograph so that, at least for the non-arable land of Scotland, it will be relatively simple to make a translation.

Implicit in Dr. Kirby's paper is the distinction, important if not complete, between the use of remote sensing for mapping purposes and for extracting land attributes on a more selective non-cartographic basis as exemplified by the Coastal Survey. I realise that I've only touched on a few of the many interesting points made by Dr. Kirby in his paper but I should like to conclude by asking him what he sees as the main gaps in land assessment on an all Scottish rather than a regional or local basis and if and how he thinks the use of remote sensing might help to fill these gaps through either a cartographic or non-cartographic, land attribute recording approach.

Reply by R.P. Kirby.

There are obvious gaps at the national level in modern maps of land cover types and land management practice. These maps might be produced in the near future from sequential satellite imagery. Such maps would be of great interest in education but I do not believe they would be of as much use for planning and management as a series of larger-scale regional maps, allowing more detailed land classifications. The non-cartographic alternatives, such as data storage on a National Grid basis for the whole of Scotland derived either from aerial photographs or from LANDSAT digital data, could provide greater quantities of more precise information but the acquisition, interrogation and presentation problems make these analytical sources much less immediately attractive, as Mr. Goodier has confirmed for the survey of Scottish Coastal Habitats.

CHAPTER 3

SOIL RESEARCH AND LAND USE CAPABILITY INTERPRETATIVE MAPS

J.S. Bibby
Soil Survey of Scotland

ABSTRACT

The emphasis in this paper is on physical characteristics of land, particularly soil
systems.   The range of soil investigations being undertaken in Scotland is reviewed,
with special reference to the Macaulay Institute;   for the widest dissemination, a
knowledge of the areal distribution of land properties is vital.   The work being
undertaken on a soil map of Scotland for publication at a scale of 1:250,000 is described, as is the prospect of a soil data bank.   Recent advances in the land-use
capability classification for agriculture are described and attention is drawn to
the problems of identifying limits significant for agriculture.   The field of
capability interpretation is still in its infancy;   the computer has an essential
part to play, especially in linking economical political aspects to physical factors.
The short-term need is for sufficient data on soil properties to permit prediction
at unvisited sites and on accurate identification of limiting characters.

KEYWORDS

Soil systems;   Macaulay Institute;   Soil map of Scotland;   capability;   classification
for agriculture;   limiting characters;   measured soil properties;   computing and
capability interpretation.

INTRODUCTION

The word *land* is subject to a wide variety of interpretations and definitions, ranging
from the purely scientific to the highly emotive.   In the context of this paper land
refers to the physical resource, a combination of factors of climate, vegetation,
landform, fauna, geologic materials and time that are expressed as soil systems.

The role of a soil research institute is to investigate the soil system and to present its findings in ways which are of use to those individuals or authorities that
have need of them.   This presentation takes a wide range of forms from papers on
matters of detail in learned journals to minor reports and conversations with non-
specialist users.   To be totally objective and accurate is the aim, a utopian ideal
never fulfilled, but there is a close relationship between the ideal situation and
the quality and quantity of the data available.

It is with this in view that this contribution examines the range of soil investigations currently being undertaken to support one form of presentation, land-use capability maps, and indicates some of the problems and future developments.

SOIL RESEARCH

The White Paper *Farming and the Nation* (Cmnd.7458), published in February 1979, stated that the rapid growth in productivity in British agriculture was due in no small mea-sure to the fruits of research, development and advice.   It focussed attention on the most pressing needs but it also considered the longer term requirement for fun-damental work arising from the need to understand some of the basic processes of animal and plant life.   The Macaulay Institute is the principal centre for soil research in Scotland and its scientific staff are engaged in both applied and basic research.

The processes active in soil formation and the properties of soil components, in par-ticular the contribution of crystalline and non-crystalline inorganic material, to-gether with the characteristics of the surfaces of particles are investigated in the Pedology Department.   A subsection of this department deals with the extent and nature of Scottish peat resources (and has a very active programme involving the use of satellite imagery in this respect), as well as investigating the cycling of nut-rients in forests.   The work of the Spectrochemistry Department is broadly divided into three fields: studies of the amount and distribution of trace elements in soils and plant material; the development of analytical methods for widening the coverage and lowering the limits of determination of significant elements; and the character-isation of inorganic and organic components of soils.

The Soil Fertility Department makes an important and direct contribution to agricul-ture through its study of crop production and soil management.   In particular, there has been a concentration on soil nutrient-crop relationships; the department is now also interested in the very important sphere of physical measurement of soils. Recent results of research have included information on the effects of weather and fertilizer placement on swedes; the timing of defoliation and the absolute and rel-ative yields of ware and seed potatoes; and chemical control of weed grasses under various techniques of cultivation in Northern Scotland, emphasising the importance of soil conditions and climatic factors in relation to husbandry.

The Department of Soil Organic Chemistry studies the nature and properties of soil organic matter and is currently concentrating its efforts on the readily-soluble components which have been shown to be important in affecting the activity of some plant enzymes.   They could also influence the availability, uptake and translocation of trace elements, and soil drainage is believed to be important.   The Plant Phys-iology Department has been conducting an investigation into the uptake of selenium by plants to assist in determining the effects of selenium deficiency on stock. The incidence of *take-all* disease in spring barley has been among the subjects studied by the Microbiology Department.

Other organisations in Scotland also conduct soil research: the Hill Farming Res-earch Organisation, the Colleges of Agriculture, the National Institute of Agricul-tural Engineering, the Forestry Commission and several university departments. Some national organisations also have programmes effective here.   Many organisations concentrate upon problems in specific fields often related to systems of use (e.g., hill farming or forestry), while others investigate the impacts of changing technol-ogy on soils (e.g., the National Institute of Agricultural Engineering).

By far the largest effort and resources are devoted to the investigation of the pro-perties and mechanics of soil and to the identification and solution of particular problems of users.   A smaller, but no less important, contribution is coming from the enquiry into the distribution of soil types and their related characteristics, for without a knowledge of the extent and location of the relevant soil properties, the translation into practice of many of the findings of soil research is difficult. The Soil Survey Department of the Macaulay Institute is charged with the classification and mapping of the soil resources of Scotland.   If the assertion is accepted that a knowledge of the distribution of soil characters is an important element in the use of information produced by soil research, an examination of the progress and programme of the survey is of interest.

SOIL SURVEY

Systematic soil survey started in Scotland in 1947 under the control of R. Glentworth. The scale chosen for the publication of maps was 1:63,360 and the format adopted was the third edition sheets of the Ordnance Survey which both Soil and Geological Surveys have adhered to since.   The programme was pursued principally in arable areas but with some hill land in the Borders, North-East Scotland and latterly the Western Highlands.   With 90 per cent of the arable land completed, discussions affecting the future programme of soil survey took place in 1976 and 1977 under the aegis of the Scottish Standing Committee on Rural Land Use, which was concerned with progress in land-use capability classification in both the lowlands and uplands.   These discussions embraced a wide range of user organisations under the chairmanship of the Chief Agricultural Officer for Scotland.   Two clearly recognisable and separate requirements were identified: a) strategic and regional information, and b) detailed local information.   As a result, from the spring of 1979 a major part of the resources of the Soil Survey Department is being devoted to a reconnaissance in pursuits of the requirements for strategic information and to complete a first-stage coverage of soil maps cover of Scotland.   This cover will be complete by 1982 when soil maps at a scale of 1:250,000 will be published.   On the basis of the reconnaissance, further detailed mapping with priorities determined by major users will take place.   The reconnaissance will also provide a strong basis for national correlation of soil types.

THE 1:250,000 MAPPING PROGRAMME

The soil maps will be published in the format outlined in Fig. 3.1.   An extract from a draft of sheet 4 is given in Fig. 3.2 to indicate the general appearance and level of detail.   Each sheet will be accompanied by a descriptive handbook and by maps at the same scale showing land capability for agriculture and for forestry. The units on the soil maps will, of necessity, be complex (i.e., each will consist of two or more soil types), but the methods of description and soil classification will be similar to those currently in use to enable cross-referencing to more detailed work where this is available.   In particular, the concept of the soil association will be retained.   The association is a group of defined and named soil units (series and complexes), regularly associated geographically in a defined proportional pattern.   Since the geological and geomorphological properties of land in Scotland are usually well-expressed, there is an in-built emphasis on the soil parent material and on defined land types.

In the arable areas of the country, the mapping will be, as far as possible, a reduction of the published information at the 1:63,360 scale with complex units introduced where matters of scale and clear cartographic presentation make this necessary. An investigation conducted by Ragg and Henderson (1979) in West Lothian has shed light on the variation of soil map units designed for 1:63,360 mapping in the till plain (Table 3.1).   They concluded that soil series map units show considerable internal variation in terms of percentages of different soils but that the soils are so similar in their most important characteristics that they do not significantly affect the pattern of use.

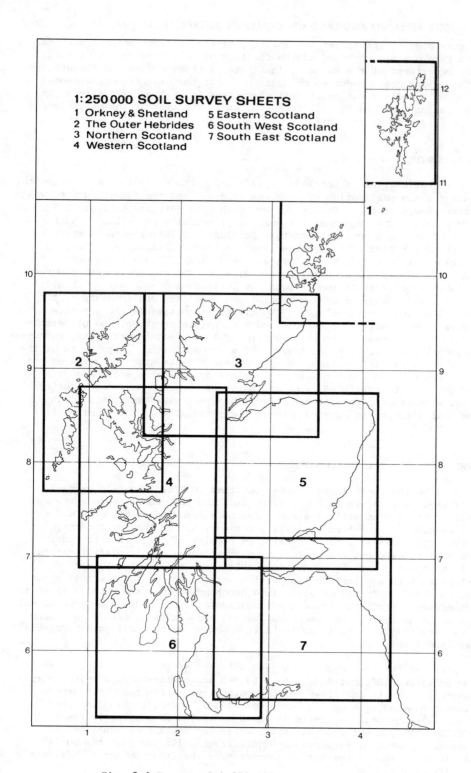

1:250 000 SOIL SURVEY SHEETS
1 Orkney & Shetland 5 Eastern Scotland
2 The Outer Hebrides 6 South West Scotland
3 Northern Scotland 7 South East Scotland
4 Western Scotland

Fig. 3.1 Format of 1:250,000 Soil Survey Sheets

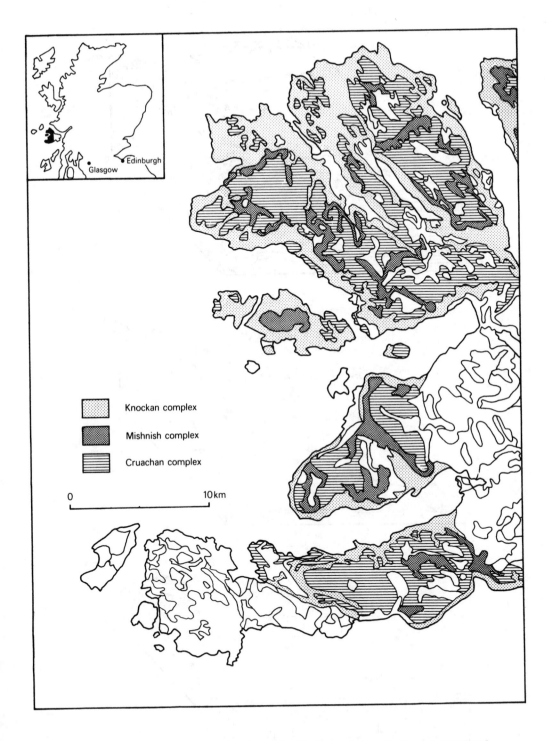

Fig. 3.2 Extract from First Draft Map of the Soils of Scotland
(Sheet 4, Western Scotland, Scale 1:250,000)

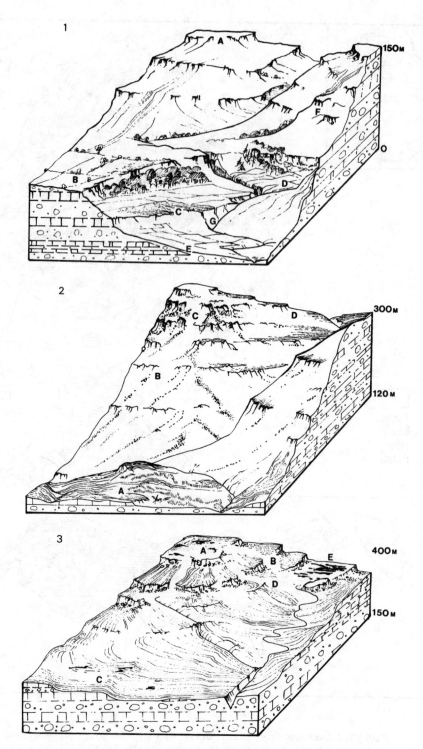

Fig. 3.3 Schematic Diagrams of Three Soil Complexes within
Darleith Association

1   Knockan Soil Complex

This complex exhibits the strong terrace topography characteristic of the plateau basalts of north-west Scotland and
is dominated by brown forest soils (table 2). The principal elements of its pattern are the scarp slopes with small
crags and vegetated debris fans (A), contrasting sharply
with dip slopes covered by colluvial drift (B). Shallow
soils predominate and may be on rocky knolls (D) or in
fields (E) or they may even be peaty at scarp edges (C).
Slopes too steep for improvement but with good quality
grazings (F) are separated on land use capability maps.
Streams are frequently incised in their lower courses (G).

2   Mishnish Soil Complex

This complex is usually found at greater elevations than
Knockan complex. Peaty knolls with rock close to the surface and deeper freely drained soils in hollows form an
intergrade with it (A). The predominant podzolic soils
(table 2) are found on steeper slopes (B) which may have
areas of more pronounced rock outcrop (C). Where slope
declines, especially at higher elevations, peaty gley soils
develop (D) forming intergrades to Cruachan complex.

3   Cruachan Soil Complex

Cruachan complex is also found at higher elevations than
Knockan complex and on more gentle slopes than Mishnish
complex. Dominated by peat and peaty gley soils (table 2)
it has several variants. Rocky areas with peat erosion (A),
especially in the upper oroboreal zone, are often associated
with strong terracing and limited drier scarp slopes of
scree (B). Terrace topography without much rock outcrop is
characteristic of lower elevations (C) and in some areas
peat erosion may occur (E). Strong flushing in broad
channels is characteristic (D).

TABLE 3.1 Percentages of Various Taxonomic Units Within Four
Mapping Units (West Lothian)

Mapping Units

Taxonomic Unit	Rowanhill	Caprington	Aberdona	Macmerry
		Percentage of unit		
Aberdona[1]	14.2	16.1	52.8	5.6
Caprington[1]	6.9	42.9	13.8	13.9
Macmerry[1]	2.5	14.3	4.1	51.4
Rowanhill[2]	65.9	10.7	12.2	8.3
Darvel[3]	0.5	3.6	4.1	12.5
Colluvial soils	3.6	7.1	4.1	2.8
Other units	6.4	5.4	8.9	5.6

1 = imperfectly-drained brown forest soils
2 = poorly-drained non-calcareous gley soil
3 = freely-drained brown forest soil

Source: Ragg and Henderson (1979).

Map units in the uplands will be more complex, principally because of the intricate patterns of the terrain (Fig. 3.3).   Bibby (1979) has studied the variation contained in mapping units in Argyllshire and concluded that, while there is variation of a similar order to that reported by Ragg and Henderson from the lowlands, the differences between soil types are much more marked (Table 3.2).   However, these differences serve only to complement strong limitations imposed on the use of the soils by other factors such as climate and site characteristics and, like the map units reported from West Lothian, those in Argyllshire also form useful vehicles for carrying statements about potential land use.   A conclusion reached by all the authors is that not all map units are equally variable, and in subsequent detailed mapping, some map separates will require more study than others, depending on the ease with which clearly-defined field recognition characters can be established.

In order to check the variation of soils throughout Scotland, the Soil Survey has started to compile a soil data bank, based initially upon 3,200 intersects of the national grid (5 km interval).   Approximately 800 of these sites will be sampled for laboratory analysis, the remainder being subjected to morphological, site and vegetation assessments only.   Since the Soil Survey of England and Wales has also embarked upon a similar scheme, a soil data bank for Great Britain should eventually be available.

INTERPRETATION

At the end of the last war the Department of Agriculture for Scotland established a system for grading the arable land of the country.   The classification was undertaken by officers of the department and the work they did then is still in use today. It represented an advance over the maps of current land use prepared by Stamp just prior to the war.   In the early 1970s, however, the Scottish Standing Committee on Rural Land Use decided to review land capability mapping in Scotland and, after lengthy deliberation by two working parties and a technical group, accepted recommendations that the classification of land-use capability as developed in the mid-1960s for use in Great Britain should become the principal document for land planning. In view of this, the Macaulay Institute, using the soil survey maps as a base, has been producing interpretative maps for agriculture.   Consultation between the Department of Agriculture and the Macaulay Institute is now good and consistently being improved to make the best use of research facilities, and the Colleges of Agriculture, through the agronomic expertise of their advisory staffs, also play a

TABLE 3.2 Percentages of Various Taxonomic Units Within Three
Mapping Units (Argyllshire)

	Mapping Unit		
Taxonomic Unit	Knockan complex	Mishnish complex	Cruachan complex
	Percentage of unit		
Brown forest soil	76	8	0
Humus iron podzol	2	39	0
Peaty gley podzol	1	16	14
Humic gley	1	2	2
Peaty gley	1	16	25
Brown ranker	11	3	1
Peaty ranker	0	7	7
Peat	1	2	45
Alluvium	3	2	0
Rock	2	3	7
Other	2	2	0

Source: Bibby (1979).

large part.   Land-use capability maps now supplement the use of the Department's own scheme which will eventually be superseded.

The land-use capability system is based on the principle of limiting factors which are expressed as guidelines.   Attention is drawn to the fact that guidelines are not rigid rules to be observed in every circumstance; the complexities of the subject do not allow that, but it is expected that any deviation from them be fully explained in texts and reports in the interests of standardisation.   Guidelines are the responsibility of a technical committee under the auspices of the Agricultural Development and Advisory Service but augmented by representatives from the Department of Agriculture and the Scottish Agricultural Colleges, the Meteorological Office and the Soil Surveys of England and Wales and Scotland.   Negotiations with the Ministry of Agriculture in England and Wales are proceeding and it can be confidently predicted that the Ministry's classification, which is used in England but not in Scotland, will be incorporated so that a single classification will emerge.

Since the land-use capability system was published (Bibby and Mackney, 1969) considerable testing of the published guidelines by application has taken place.   Much of this has highlighted the lack of detailed information, not only on the characteristics of land but also on the way in which specific land features influence use.   An example of the former is the lack of weather-recording stations in hill areas and of information on soils; of the latter the lack of measured data on how slope affects implements.   Although the National Institute of Agricultural Engineering has studied the problem (Spencer and Gilfillan, 1976), the results are theoretical rather than practical.

Some improvements have, however, been made.   Subsequent to the publication by the Macaulay Institute of maps assessing climatic conditions in Scotland (Birse and Dry, 1970; Birse and Robertson, 1970; Birse, 1971) an interpretation was developed for use in Scotland in terms of classes in the land classification system (Bibby, 1977, Fig. 3.4).   Work is now being undertaken by the Meteorological Office to improve these (Francis, 1979).   Guidelines applying to soil criteria are currently being revised and methods of ranking subclasses have been requested, particularly for land in classes 3, 5 and 6.   Lack of space precludes a full discussion of these developments but since land use in large areas of Scotland is dominated by potential conflicts between farming and forestry, it may be helpful to review the methods currently

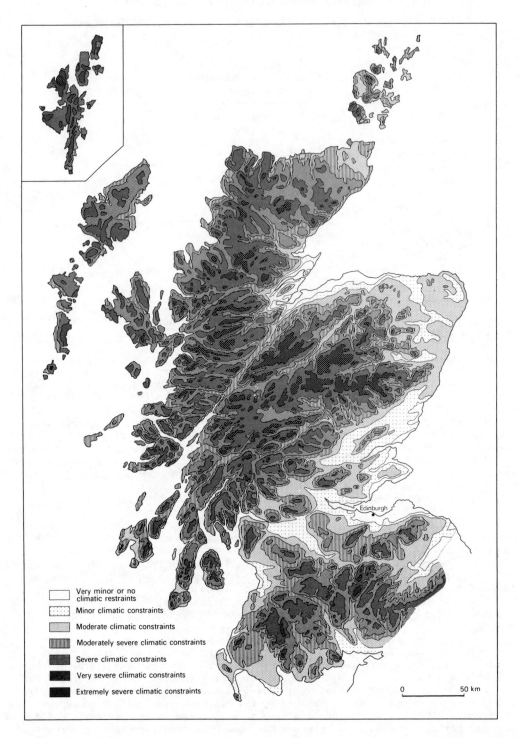

Fig. 3.4 Assessment of Climatic Factors in Land Use Capability Classification for Agriculture in Scotland. Based on maps of accumulated temperature above 5.6°C, potential water deficit and exposure (Birse, Dry and Robertson, 1970).

being used to give information on grazing capability for sheep in Class 6.

Class 6 is currently defined as that land which cannot be improved by the use of mechanised methods but which has a value for grazing.   It is clear that the class therefore ranges from steep slopes at low altitude, with a very useful semi-natural grassland, to poor rough grazing at high altitudes.   The key to assessment is the existing vegetation cover and the phytosociological work of McVean and Ratcliffe (1962) and of Birse and Robertson (1976) is of great value.   By working out ratings for plant communities according to a system described for Germany by Klapp and others (1953) and adjusted for Scottish conditions by the Soil Survey in consultation with the Hill Farming Research Organisation, general relativities may be established and the vegetation classed in one of three groups of relative grazing values.   The method was used in a crude form for the Highlands and Islands Development Board's Survey of the Isle of Mull (HIDB, 1973) and has since been refined, as is shown in Table 3.3 (Robertson, 1979).   The varying use of plant communities by grazing animals is under investigation by the Hill Farming Research Organisation and provides severe diffic- ulties in assessment; but, as a first approximation, the system described is satis- factory.

TABLE 3.3 Ordering of Grassland and Moorland Communities in Terms of Their Grazing Value to Sheep

	Community	Grazing Class	Grazing Value
1.	Permanent and old ley pastures	Good	11.75
2.	Rotational ley pastures	Good	10.80
3.	Crested hair-grass grassland	Good	7.40
4.	Meadow-grass - bent grassland	Good	7.10
5.	Rich bent-fescue grassland	Good	6.60
6.	Upland bent-fescue grassland	Good	6.50
7.	Milk-vetch - red fescue dune	Good	5.90
8.	Acid bent-fescue grassland	Good	5.70
9.	Bent-fescue grassland with bracken	Good	5.45
10.	Heath-grass - white bent grassland	Good	5.40
11.	Sharp-flowered rush pasture	Good	5.15
12.	Eyebright - red fescue dune	Good	5.00
13.	Soft rush pasture	Good	4.80
14.	Rock-rose - fescue grassland	Good	4.80
15.	White bent grassland	Good	4.60
16.	Flying bent grassland	Moderate	3.90
17.	Herb-rich atlantic heather moor	Moderate	2.50
18.	Herb-rich boreal heather moor	Moderate	2.15
19.	Bog moss water track	Poor	1.65
20.	Dry atlantic heather moor	Poor	1.45
21.	Moist atlantic heather moor	Poor	1.45
22.	Northern atlantic heather moor	Poor	1.40
23.	Northern bog heather moor	Poor	1.05
24.	Northern blanket bog	Poor	1.05
25.	Blanket bog	Poor	0.95
26.	Dry boreal heather moor	Poor	0.90
27.	Bog heather moor	Poor	0.90
28.	Mountain blanket bog	Poor	0.90
29.	Moist boreal heather moor	Poor	0.85
30.	Lichen-rich boreal heather moor	Poor	0.85
31.	Blanket bog - terminal phase	Poor	0.50

Source: Robertson, J.S. (1979).

Land-use capability maps for agriculture, in one form or another, are commonplace in a world context.   The last five years in Great Britain has seen a widening interest in other forms of interpretation.   Some of these are related to specific aspects of agriculture.   A system for classying land according to its suitability for grass-land is being developed by Harrod; soil suitability maps for direct drilling have also been made.   In England and Wales a map showing the potential of land to accept rain in winter has been made for the Institute of Hydrology from information on soils. As a result of the recommendations of a working party of the Scottish Standing Committee on Rural Land Use, the Macaulay Institute is cooperating with the Forestry Commission on the production of a land capability system for forestry.

The field of capability interpetation is still in its infancy.   Major future devel-opments will include improved methods of collecting field data in many disciplines and better linkage of the results to information derived from research.   Because of the large amounts of data and the complex interactive processes involved, the computer has an essential and increasing role to play, particularly in linking the relatively ephemeral economic and political aspects of the physical basis of land use.

Nevertheless, the short-term emphasis must be on the acquisition of a sufficient quantity and quality of measured soil and site properties to allow confident predic-tion of conditions at unvisited sites.   Accurate identification of limiting charac-ters for various uses must also be achieved.   This combination of sound observation of site properties and knowledge of limited characters will enable us to be much more precise in future evaluation of the alternative uses of land.

REFERENCES

Agricultural Ministers, (1979). *Farming and the Nation,* Cmnd. 7458, HMSO, London.
Bibby, J.S. (1977), *Assessment of Climatic Factors in Land Use Capability Classifi-cation for Agriculture in Scotland* (map). Unpublished, Macaulay Institute, Aberdeen.
Bibby, J.S., (in press), Soil survey and its interpretation for agriculture in the West Highlands.   In *Proceedings of the Welsh Soils Discussion Group*.
Bibby, J.S. and D. Mackney, (1969). *Land Use Capability Classification,* Tech. Mono. 1, The Soil Survey, Macaulay Institute, Aberdeen.
Birse, E.L., (1971). *Assessment of Climatic Conditions in Scotland,* No. 3. The Bioclimatic sub-regions, Macaulay Institute, Aberdeen.
Birse, E.L. and F. Dry, (1970). *Assessment of Climatic Conditions in Scotland,* No. 1, based on accumulated temperature and potential water deficit, Macaulay Institute, Aberdeen.
Birse, E.L. and L. Robertson, (1970). *Assessment of Climatic Conditions in Scotland,* No.2, based on exposure and accumulated frost, Macaulay Institute, Aberdeen.
Birse, E.L. and J.S. Robertson, (1976). *Plant Communities and Soils of the Lowland and Southern Upland Regions of Scotland.*   Monograph. Soil Survey of Scotland, Macaulay Institute, Aberdeen.
Francis, P.E., (in press). Some climatic factors in land assessment.   In M.F. Thomas and J.T. Coppock (Eds) *Land Assessment in Scotland*.
HIDB, (1973). *Island of Mull - Survey and Proposals for Development.*   Special Report No. 10, Highlands and Islands Development Board, Inverness.
Klapp, F., P. Boeker, F. Konig, and A. Stahlin, (1953). Wertzahlen der Grunlandpflan-zen, *Das Grunland Nr. 5,* M. and H. Schaper, Hannover.
McVean, D.N. and D.A. Ratcliffe, (1962). *Plant Communities of the Scottish Highlands,* Monograph 1, Nature Conservancy, HMSO, London.
Ragg, J.M. and R. Henderson, (1979). A reappraisal of soil mapping in an area of southern Scotland.   Parts I and II.   *Journ. Soil Sci.* (submitted).
Robertson, J.S., (1979). Ordering of grassland and moorland communities in terms of their relative grazing value for sheep, Papers from a course in vegetation survey-ing (unpublished).   Macaulay Institute, Aberdeen.

DISCUSSION

Comment by D.A. Davidson, University of Strathclyde.

It is 10 years since the scheme for land use capability classification by Bibby and Mackney (1969) was published and we are grateful to Mr. Bibby for reviewing the work done on this topic and for indicating current research by the staff of the Soil Survey of Scotland. At the international level major advances have also been made in recent years, best expressed in the FAO *Framework for Land Evaluation*. This document, the result of much international discussion over several years, provides a clear methodological framework for land assessment for defined land uses.

There is no doubt that when the new 1:250,000 sheets are published they will be useful for national and regional rural land use planning, but I wonder if the Soil Survey should also be devising methods for the production of a broader range of interpretative maps at the local scale. The example which springs to my mind is the situation of applied soil survey in the Netherlands. For that country coverage by 1:200,000 soil and soil suitability maps was completed by 1970, but the need for more detailed maps for land use planning was always recognised. The Netherlands Soil Survey Institute has produced much publicity material illustrating how large scale soils maps can be interpreted in terms of several land uses. Some examples are interpretations for such uses as arable land, pasture, forestry, building construction and sportsfields. In addition Dutch soil surveyors become actively involved in the planning of land use through the land consolidation schemes. The Dutch work demonstrates the value of a flexible approach to land assessment, the advantages of applied soil survey work at detailed scales and the merits of publicity exercises. Some American states now run soil survey education programmes. American studies are also available to demonstrate the clear cost benefits of a soil survey in an area prior to urban development.

Mr. Bibby very rightly concludes that the topic of capability interpretation is still in its infancy, but I am suggesting that in the next decade attention should be given to the local as well as to the regional and national scales, a point also made by Professor Coppock. It is only at the local level that the value of soil data to land use matters can be clearly demonstrated. Surely this is now possible at least for lowland Scotland with 90 per cent of the arable area now mapped? Has the time not arrived when the staff of the Soil Survey ought to be giving greater publicity to their achievements so that they can be more involved with land use matters at the local level?

Comment by R.P.C. Morgan, National College of Agricultural Engineering, Silsoe.

I would like to reinforce the comments made by Dr. Davidson in that, on looking through the abstracts of the papers for this symposium, no mention is made of the work on land assessment by FAO or the Dutch workers. It is recognised in the approaches of both these groups that fundamental assessments of the physical resources of an area must be kept separate from the economic and social factors which finally influence the suitability of land for specific uses. The land capability classification as such is only a partial answer to an appraisal of the physical attributes of the land. Its emphasis on limitations of the land for use provides important information for planning but this type of analysis needs to be paralleled by a more positive study of land qualities. Land capability assessment should be divided into two parts: land quality and land sensitivity which would be based on the limitations for use and the degradation of land likely to result from misuse. Any assessment of land must provide a base for determining what the land can be used for and predicting the environmental consequences of use or misuse, otherwise it has no practical value.

Reply by J.S. Bibby.

Three principal points have been raised in discussion.   These are.
1. the adoption of another system for land evaluation (FAO or a land *quality* structure),
2. the requirement for a broader range of maps at local scales,
3. the need for publicity, education and involvement in land planning.

The Land Use Capability Classification as adopted for British use is a method of land
assessment that has been widely used throughout the world and has proved to be adapt-
able to a variety of circumstances.   It is my belief that it is strongest for use
in planning exercises at the national or regional level, when a general picture is
required.   Three paths are available for more detailed information; firstly to develop the existing land capability classification to the unit level as has been done
by Soil Survey of England and Wales; secondly to devise suitability maps for specific
crops or agricultural operations (Cannell and others, 1978; Pidgeon and Ragg, 1979);
or thirdly to define specific land uses and to classify physical data accordingly
(Brinkman and Smyth, 1973).   Increasing detail in the level of classification requires increasing detail in the quality and quantity of observations at all levels
and this cannot be achieved overnight in the real world of financial limits.   In
Scotland, a phased and structured approach to these problems is being made by the
Soil Survey and, as I indicated in my paper, it is fully intended to widen the scope
and range of interpretations in the future.   This will inevitably involve more publicity and education, greater resources for this work together with more active co-
operation between all research workers to make the best use of those currently
available.

REFERENCES

Brinkman, R., and J.A. Smyth (Ed), (1973). Publ. 17, Wageningen;   Intern. Inst. Land
    Reclam. and Improvement (ILRI).
Cannell, R.Q., D.B. Davies, D. Mackney, and J.D. Pidgeon, (1978). Outlook Agric. Vol.
    9, 306.
Pidgeon, J.D., and J.M. Ragg, (1979). Outlook Agric. Vol.10, 49.

CHAPTER 4
SOME CLIMATIC FACTORS IN LAND ASSESSMENT

P.E. Francis
Agricultural Unit, Meteorological Office

ABSTRACT

Over the past fifteen years a series of publications has developed the theme of
climatological factors in land assessment.   The most widely-used climatological
parameters have been temperature and rainfull, whether as basic variables or processed in some way.   The approach is adopted that the physiological requirements
of crops in their early stages, plus periods of access by machines and animals,
provide a valid matrix of conditions.   Recent work shows that the most temperature-
sensitive period is leaf production in spring, which occurs at temperatures as low
as 0°C; accumulated temperatures over 0°C from January to June are therefore used.
Machines and animals can cause damage when soils are wet, and the balance between
rainfall and evaporation can be presented in terms of an accessibility period.
The growing volume of data on magnetic tape permits much more flexible use, but the
work on land assessment is at a formative stage and a tabular presentation of results
is preferred to a map.

KEYWORDS

Choice of parameters;   leaf formation stage;   accessibility period;   accumulated
day degrees;   short-term averages;   inter quartile range.

INTRODUCTION

The zonation of the British Isles by means of climatic parameters has been the subject of much work by many authors.   The emphasis of such work has not usually been
on land assessment, but the climatic parameters chosen and the classification techniques used have provided a useful resource for work on land assessment.   Previous
work can be divided into general geographical treatments (e.g., Sharaf, 1954;
Gregory, 1976) and into classifications with a definite purpose in mind, e.g.,
forestry (Fairbairn, 1968) and botany (Birse and Dry, 1970;   Birse and Robertson,
1970;   Birse, 1971a).   Recent advances in techniques of automatic data processing
have enabled mathematical pattern analysis to be undertaken, and this is now a
growing field of activity (Steiner, 1965;   McBoyle, 1972;   Ayoade, 1977).

Climatic classification primarily designed for land assessment was probably first
considered in Great Britain by the Agricultural Land Service of the Ministry of
Agriculture, Fisheries & Food (1966).   Since that time there has been a gradual

addition to the knowledge of the subject, and an overall improvement in techniques of classification (Bibby and Mackney, 1969; Birse, 1971a; Bendelow and Hartnup, 1977).   The archiving of climatological data on magnetic tape by the Meteorological Office has made the task of accessing and processing such data much simpler than it was, and consequently a more versatile use of data is now possible.

The purpose of this contribution is to discuss climatic factors suitable for use in the classification of land for agricultural purposes.   Past classifications based on climate, whether designed for general or agricultural purposes, have made use of the two climatic variables, temperature and rainfull.   The temperature element has been presented in a variety of ways, either as a primary variable such as a summer maximum value (Bibby and Mackney, 1969), or in a processed form.   Two such forms are length of growing season, defined as that part of the year for which mean daily air temperatures are above a critical value (Sharaf, 1954; Fairbairn, 1968), and an even less fundamental variable, accumulated day degrees (Thom, 1966).   Accumulated day degrees approximate the total *energy* above a given critical threshold and have been used by agronomists and heating engineers for many years.   The use of accumulated day degrees in climatic classification has been quite general (Sharaf, 1954; Birse and Dry, 1970; Birse, 1971b; Bendelow and Hartnup, 1977), and the accepted critical value in this instance, as well as for length of growing season, has usually been 42°F or 6°C.

The other generally-used parameter in climatic classifications is wetness or dryness. This factor can be presented as total rainfall (Fairbairn, 1968), sometimes complemented by information on altitude (Ministry of Agriculture, 1966; Bibby and Mackney, 1969), or in a processed form.   In recent years the balance between rainfall and evaporation has been used as an agriculturally significant parameter (Bibby and Mackney, 1969; Birse and Dry, 1970; Bendelow and Hartnup, 1977), and other more involved indices have also been employed (Sharaf, 1954).

THE RATIONALE FOR SELECTING CLIMATIC FACTORS IN LAND ASSESSMENT

The choice of climatic parameters in an agricultural land assessment, or any other classification, implies a resulting zonation of the land area being studied.   To be of any real value, that zonation should accord with any existing and well-established pattern of land use.   The problem then arises how best to select the original climatic factors so that the final zonation is both realistic and easily interpreted. A solution to the problem is to consider the climatic limitations that can easily be identified for particular agricultural practices and crops.   The physiological requirements for high crop yields are fairly well understood (Waring and Cooper, 1971; Biscoe and Gallagher, 1977), and one obvious climatic factor is early season warmth. The use of accumulated day degrees, as noted earlier, is a well-tried method of climatological classification.   However, the usual *base* value of 6°C (42°-43°F) has only historical support.   Recent work (Peacock, 1975a, 1975b; Biscoe and Gallagher, 1978) has shown that grass and cereals maintain leaf growth, albeit slowly, down to 0°C, and this value can thus be safely used as a base value for accumulation of temperatures.   Past classifications have also considered such accumulations over the entire year or through a notional growing season.   The consensus of recent work on crop physiology is that temperature is most important during leaf growth, and even that high temperatures in late summer adversely affect yield by hastening the senescence of leaves and by raising rates of respiration (Waring and Cooper, 1971).

A climatic parameter that expresses the balance between rainfall and evaporation is an obvious choice for inclusion into an agricultural classification, but that parameter should be capable of easy interpretation in terms of farming practice.   A straight-forward accumulation of difference between evaporation and rainfall gives an estimate of maximum values of soil moisture deficit in the summer (Birse and Dry, 1970; Bendelow and Hartnup, 1977).   Such an estimate has, however, to be modified by the soil-crop combinations that are possible, and the economics of irrigation in drier areas introduces a complicating factor.   Ideally, a parameter of climatic moisture balance should be quantifiable in unequivocal terms that can be directly related to crop needs or alternatively to the optimal management of the land.   A parameter that should be considered is the *accessibility period* or number of days in a year when either machinery can work on the land or animals can use pasture without damaging the sward.   Earliness and lateness of access are important factors in all types of farming.   In the spring, early access permits preparation of a good seed-bed, early sowing and establishment, and hence a high leaf area when maximum amounts of radiation occur in mid-summer.   The decline in yield of most arable crops owing to late sowing is quite marked and makes an early start to the season very important.   Late return to field capacity in the autumn facilitates easy harvesting, cultivation of stubbles for weed control and a longer season in which sugar beet and late-sown crops can mature.   Livestock farmers who rely on good grassland management benefit equally from good access.   A relatively early departure from field capacity enables stock to be turned out onto grass early, so saving on winter food. Good management requires early application of fertiliser, more than one cut of hay/silage and, in good years, the ability to make use of any autumn regrowth.   Very short or broken periods of accessibility indicate areas suitable only for rough grazing since improvement would be impossible without the use of machinery and damage by poaching would be highly likely.

PRESENTATION OF DATA

The mode of presentation of data, once the individual parameters have been chosen, is also open to debate.   Most previous classifications have used mean values of climatic parameters, and the possibilities of using more distributional information have been largely ignored, with a few exceptions (Gregory, 1976).   The difficulty of processing large amounts of data by hand is a partial explanation for this general omission, and the easier access to climatological data, mentioned earlier, provides an opportunity to present a different analysis of the basic data.   The comprehension of a climatic classification is made easier by presentation of the results in the form of a map or maps.   Immediate problems can then occur, since for most practical purposes, e.g., land assessment, large-scale maps are required which stretch the validity of the climatological information that is being presented. For example, maps to the scale 1:625,000 (Birse and Dry, 1970; Birse and Robertson, 1970; Birse, 1971a) are heavily biased towards a topographical extrapolation rather than to a known climatological picture.   On the other hand, smaller scales such as 1:8,000,000 can be of only very limited value (Fairbairn, 1968).   The work reported in this chapter is at a preliminary stage and it would be misleading to try to present the results obtained so far in map form.

Another important point to consider is the question of possible climatic variation and the degree to which a climatological classification is representative for a point in time outside of the period over which the contributing data were collected. Various climatological publications (Meteorological Office, 1976, 1977; Ordnance Survey, 1967) illustrate the small changes in average temperature and rainfull between different averaging periods, and the implication is that a current climatological classification would be applicable as long as no very large climatic change occurred.

A PROPOSED CLASSIFICATION

The climatic classification proposed in this paper is based on the reasoning outlined earlier and on the two concepts of early season warmth and accessibility during the whole farming year.   The picture of Scotland that emerges is essentially no different from that illustrated by previous work orientated towards land assessment (Birse, 1971b), but the relationship between Scotland and southern England, for example, is put into

a completely different light.   The choice of climatological parameters for an agricultural classification should bear some relationship to the observed agricultural
performance in the areas being examined.   It is worth noticing that Scottish wheat
and barley yields are higher than those in England and Wales (Ministry of Agriculture and others, 1977) and that, for these crops, it would appear that the cooler,
less dry, Scottish climate is more beneficial than is the hotter and drier climate
of parts of south and east England.   The use of yearly accumulated day-degrees ac-
centuates the differences in the maximum summer temperatures that can be experienced
in eastern Scotland and the south-east of England.   Half year totals above 0°C, as
well as covering the initial period of leaf extension, exclude the hottest months
of July and August in which the less maritime areas of southern England can experience relatively high maximum values of temperature.   As an illustration, the Cambridge area can, on average, accumulate around 2000 day degrees above a base value
of 6°C in a year, whereas the average for Edinburgh is only 1450, a difference of
550 units.   Values above 0°C over 6 months, January to June, give 1500 and 1350 day
degrees respectively, i.e., a difference of only 150 units.   The climatic difference
is real, but the agriculturally significant difference can be exaggerated by an in-
judicious choice of parameter.   As already noted, the high late summer temperatures
can be disadvantageous, especially as they are usually accompanied by very dry soil
conditions and water stress in plants.
The last point leads to the question of soil water and how best to represent the
agriculturally-crucial balance between rainfall and evaporation.   Maximum summer
potential soil water deficit has been used, but once again this parameter emphasises
a climatic difference that hides the true agricultural significance.   The east of
Scotland has an agricultural advantage over the west in that the generally lower
rainfall regime allows more cultivation and less risk of leaching of fertiliser, for
instance.   This difference in wetness is shown very well by a consideration of the
maximum potential soil water deficit in summer, but when the same parameter is
applied to the very dry areas of eastern central England the answer must be interpreted in a different manner.   The large deficits are now a positive disadvantage,
crop yields can be adversely affected and the economics of irrigation can confuse
the situation.

The use of maximum potential soil water deficit in summer, and of yearly totals of
accumulated day degrees above bases other than 0°C, could be justified in schemes
of secondary classification, e.g., in designating areas suitable for forage maize
(Carr and Hough, 1978), or in identifying areas where irrigation should be considered if drought-susceptible crops are being cultivated.   The parameters suggested in
this contribution have been chosen as being agriculturally significant in that they
can be applied throughout the United Kingdom without unduly emphasising the characteristics of any one area in an ambiguous or misleading fashion.

                    EXAMPLES OF THE PROPOSED SYSTEM

The data used in the examples presented below are taken from the 20-year period 1956
to 1975 (Table 4.1).   This period includes both very wet and very day years, and a
range of mean spring and summer temperatures.   The data are taken from 11 observing
stations in north east, east and south Scotland, illustrating the range of agricultural climates that exists.   The stations used are listed in Table 4.1, together
with National Grid Reference and height.

The totals of accumulated day degrees were calculated from daily values of maximum
and minimum temperature, using a well-established technique (Meteorological Office,
1976).   The base value used was 0°C and totals were taken over the months from
January to June.

TABLE 4.1 : Total Day Degrees and Lengths of Accessibility
Period, Exceeded 3 Years in 4 at Various Locations
in Scotland

Location	National Grid Reference	Height (m)	Day Degree Total (C°)	Access Period (days)
Kinloss	38/067627	5	1187	214
Turnhouse	36/159739	35	1232	198
Leuchars	37/468209	10	1178	205
Prestwick	26/369261	16	1293	175
Abbotsinch	26/480667	5	1307	166
Dyce	38/883125	58	1097	174
Dumfries	25/982747	49	1236	151
Penicuik	36/233599	189	1096	163
Wick	39/364522	36	1057	160
Blyth Bridge	36/141463	253	1051	149
Eskdalemuir	36/235026	242	1042	89

Source: Meteorological Office, Edinburgh, data from period 1956 to 1975.

The accessibility period that is calculated from available data on rainfall and
evaporation, is very much a function of the soil moisture extraction model that is
employed.   The model used here is one for grass (Smith, 1971), but the qualitative
picture that emerges would be reflected by the results of any consistently-applied
model.   By the same reasoning, differences in soil texture and water-holding properties are also ignored, and a maximum moisture deficit of 125mm is assumed.
The daily moisture balance for each station was calculated for the 20 year period
from January 1st, 1956, with a zero moisture deficit.   Because of the difficulty
of identifying a unique point in spring from which to date the start of an accessibility period, an arbitrary value of 5 mm was taken as the critical soil moisture
deficit.   The return to field capacity in the autumn is much less difficult to
identify, since in most years autumnal rain is more than sufficient to replenish the
deficit and keep pace with evaporation and transpiration.   In the west of Scotland,
and during very wet years in the east, there are occasions when a return to field
capacity takes place during the summer, and then another drying period occurs before
the usual return to capacity in autumn.   When this sequence occurs, the wet periods
are discounted and the length of the accessibility period consequently diminished.
Field capacity, as used in this description, is defined as the maximum amount of
water held by the soil against gravity, e.g., that left after drainage of any excess.

The values shown in Table 4.1 are those which are exceeded three years in four.
This mode of presentation gives more insight into the risk involved in following a
certain farming practice, since mean values over a period can mask very different
distributional features.   For instance, over the 20 year-period, the inter-quartile
range of lengths of the accessibility-period at Dumfries is 36 days, while at Kinloss,
Leuchars and Turnhouse it is more than 80 days.   The inter-quartile range of total
accumulated day-degrees shows less variation between stations, the lowest being 108
units at Blyth Bridge, and the highest 188 units at Leuchars.   The general picture
is that the warmer areas have a relatively higher variability in total day degrees,
while the drier areas generally have a higher variability in the length of the accessibility-period.   These distributional features imply that the differences in mean
values between favoured and less-favoured areas could be misleading.

The values of total accumulated day-degrees and the lengths of the accessibility-
period likely to be exceeded three years in four are given in Table 4.1 for 11
locations in Scotland.   The values reflect the broad climatic variation in Scotland,
with warmer western areas, a decrease in temperature with an increase in latitude and

altitude, and a drier eastern region.   The stations listed in Table 4.1 are fairly representative of the areas around them, and it is interesting to compare station with station to see which regions have similar characteristics as defined by the chosen parameters.

The areas with the warmest first half of the year are coastal Ayrshire and the lower Clyde, with in excess of about 1300 units on 75 per cent of occasions.   The Lothian plain and the lowlands of Dumfriesshire total around 1230 units, while East Fife and the coastal strip of the Moray Firth accumulate about 1180 day degrees above 0°C.   The smaller totals illustrate interesting associations in that it appears that lowland Aberdeenshire and the higher ground of the Lothians have comparable totals (about 1100 units), as indeed do coastal Caithness and parts of the Southern Uplands (around 1050 units).   The range of these totals is about 20 per cent of the central value, but the length of the accessibility-period (discussed below) shows a much higher variation from one region to another.

The longest accessibility-periods occur, as would be expected, in the areas of lower rainfall in eastern Scotland.   The variation in total evaporation from north to south causes a pattern of accessibility-periods that is not, however, simply related to the distribution of annual rainfall.   The most favoured areas are the coastal strip of the Moray Firth, East Fife and East Lothian, all having an accessibility period of 200 or more days in 75 per cent of years.   It is interesting to note that lowland Aberdeenshire and coastal Ayrshire have a similar expectancy of more than 175 days, while coastal Caithness and the Lothian uplands are comparable at around 160 days. These latter areas have a difference in annual average rainfall of just over 100 mm, and Wick also has on average less rain than Prestwick or Dyce, thus illustrating how rainfall can be a misleading factor if taken on its own.   The shortest periods found among the places considered are in the Southern Uplands and in Dumfriesshire, where the higher rainfall is accompanied by relatively low evaporation rates.   The spatial variation in the length of accessibility-period is very high, the difference of the extremes being about 80 per cent of the central point of the range.

A ZONATION BASED ON THE CHOSEN PARAMETERS

The values of the selected parameters for the stations listed in Table 4.1 are presented graphically in Fig. 4.1.   The different combinations of warmth and wetness are easily seen, and the stations fall into identifiable groupings.   It is apparent that the best areas of arable farming in Scotland are categorised by the combination of warmth and dryness found in the upper right hand area of Fig. 4.1, and also that the other extreme of the agricultural spectrum is characterised by the combination found in the lower left-hand corner.   A zonation of Scotland, based on the two climatological parameters presented above, can be made by ascribing limiting values of the parameters for different types of agriculture.   An acceptable procedure would be to correlate the observed versatility of agricultural activities in an area with the corresponding position indicated on a graph, such as that of Fig. 4.1, which shows for arbitrary and regularly-spaced limits the classification of a number of individual sites.   If this were done, it would give suitable information to provide a correct delineation of climatic constraints on agricultural land use.

This approach has been undertaken by other authors in terms of land-use capability classes (Birse, 1971b) and farming types (Bendelow and Hartnup, 1977).   The latter paper is based on an analysis of farming types in England and Wales, but the climatic limits ascribed to horticulture and arable farming would appear to imply that the former was impossible in Scotland and the latter only just possible!   Birse (1971b) has a three-parameter classification, the third climatic influence being wind speed, taken as a measure of exposure.   The two-parameter model described in the main body of this paper would probably serve as a first, coarse mesh, analysis for land assessment.   On a smaller scale it would probably be necessary to bring in other climatic considerations such as exposure, risk of frost and liability to excessive soil moisture

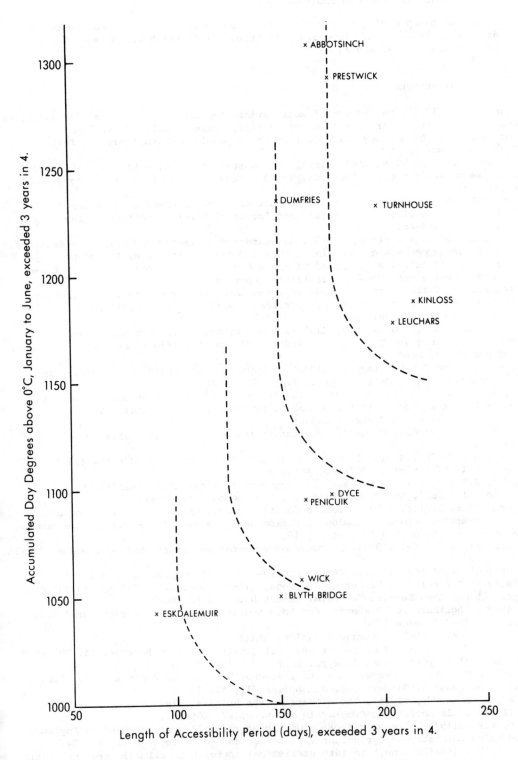

Fig. 4.1 Suggested Classification for a Limited Number of Sites

deficits.   Such sub-division in a classification would depend on local features such as topography, aspect, slope and soil type, all of which are outside the scope of a macro-climatic assessment.

REFERENCES

Ayoade, J.O., (1977). On the use of multivariate techniques in climate classification and regionalisation, *Arch. Met. Geoph. Biokl.*, Series B., 24, 257-267.

Bibby, J.S., and D. Mackney, (1969). *Land Use Capability Classification*. Soil Survey Tech. Mono. No. 1.

Bendelow, V.C., and R. Hartnup, (1977). The Assessment of climatic limitations in land use capability classification, *North of England Soil Discussion Group Proc.*, 13, 19-29.

Birse, E.L. and F.T. Dry, (1970). *Assessment of Climatic Conditions in Scotland. 1. Based on Accumulated Temperature and Potential Water Deficit*, Macaulay Institute, Aberdeen.

Birse, E.L. and L. Robertson, (1970). *Assessment of Climatic Conditions in Scotland. 2. Based on Exposure and Accumulated Frost*, Macaulay Institute, Aberdeen.

Birse, E.L., (1971a). *Assessment of Climatic Conditions in Scotland. 3. The Bio-Climatic Sub-regions*, Macaulay Institute, Aberdeen.

Birse, E.L., (1971b). Climatic assessment and land use capability classification. *Proceedings of the Field Meeting, Stirling.   Soil Survey of Scotland.* (Restricted Circulation).

Biscoe, P.V. and J.N. Gallagher, (1977). Weather, dry matter production and yield. In J.J. Landsberg and C.V. Cutting (Eds) *Environmental Effects on Crop Physiology*. Academic Press, London.

Biscoe, P.V. and J.N. Gallagher, (1978). A Physiological Analysis of Cereal Yield. 1. Production of Dry Matter, *Agric. Prog.* 53, 34-50.

Carr, M.K.V. and M.N. Hough, (1978). The influence of climate on maize production in North West Europe.   In *Forage Maize, Production and Utilisation*. Agricultural Research Council, London.

Fairbairn, W.A. (1968). Climatic zonation in the British Isles, *Forestry*, 41, (2), 117-130.

Gregory, S., (1976). Regional Climates, In T.J. Chandler and S. Gregory (Eds), *The Climate of the British Isles*, Longman, London.

McBoyle, G.R., (1972). Factor analytic approach to a climatic classification of Europe, *Clim.Bull. No.12*, McGill Univ., Dept. Geog., Montreal.

Meteorological Office, (1977). *Tables for the evaluation of daily values of accumulated temperature above and below 42°F from daily values of maximum and minimum temperature.*Met. Office Leaflet No. 10.

Meteorological Office, (1976). *Averages of temperature for the United Kingdom 1941-70.* HMSO, London.

Meteorological Office, (1977). *Annual Average Rainfall*, Met.O. 886 (NB).

Ministry of Agriculture, Fisheries and Food, (1966). *Agricultural Land Classification*. Agricultural Land Service Technical Report No.11, HMSO, London.

Ministry of Agriculture, Fisheries and Food and others, (1977). *Agricultural Statistics United Kingdom 1974*.

Ordnance Survey, (1967). *Average Annual Rainfall 1916-50*.

Peacock, J.M., (1975a). Temperature and leaf growth in Lolium Perenne. II. The site of temperature perception, *J. Appl. Ecol.* 12, 115-123.

Peacock, J.M. (1975b). Temperature and leaf growth in Lolium Perenne. III.   Factors affecting seasonal differences, *J. Appl. Ecol.*, 12, 685-697.

Sharaf, A. El-A. T., (1954). The climate of the British Isles, a new classification. *Bulletin de la Societe de Geographie d'Egypte*, 27, 209-245.

Smith, L.P., (1971). *The significance of winter rainfall over farmland in England and Wales*, Ministry of Agriculture, Fisheries and Food, Tech. Bull. No. 24.

Steiner, D., (1965). A multivariate statistical approach to climatic regionalisation and classification, Amsterdam, *Ts. K. Ned. Aard. Ge.* 82.

Thom, H.C.S., (1966). Normal degree days above any base by the Universal truncation
    coefficient, *Mon. Weath. Rev.*, 94, 461-5.
Waring, P.F. and Cooper, P.J., (1971) (Eds). *Potential Crop Production*, Heinemann.

DISCUSSION

Comment by F.H.W. Green, University of Oxford.

It is my pleasure to thank Dr. Francis for his explanation of the modern approach to
assessment of the climatic side of land use potential.

My first comment is to observe how perceptive were some of our predecessors, at a
time when they could not quantify or explain some of the climatic features, which -
by trial and error - they were evidently aware of.   For instance, early west High-
landers knew that they could not grow crops, in an area where precipitation exceeded
potential evaporation almost continuously, without ridging the land into *lazy beds*.
They also knew, incidentally, that less effort was needed on limestone; one can,
for instance, trace more olden agriculture on the Durness Limestone, in the north-
west, than on other geological formations.   Later, those who could put things down
in writing (as in the Board of Agriculture county reports at about the end of the
18th century) exhibited pretty sound ideas on the inter-relationships of soil type
and climate.   In the early part of this century, the work on defining so-called
natural regions was a great step forward in appreciation of land-use potential and
had some quantitative backing.   We may cite the work of Dudley Stamp's First Land
Utilisation Survey, in this country, in which the climatic factors affecting different land uses were given prominence, and which gave a lead to the agricultural land
services of DAFS and MAFF.

Secondly, I think that perhaps not enough attention has been given to classifying
land according to its *flexibility* of land use.   Some land can be used for many different purposes, other land cannot.   A very obvious case is that, whereas housing
estates can be built on land of fairly high relief, airfields cannot.   On the climatic side, land use is much more flexible where, in summer, potential evaporation
exceeds precipitation, than where the reverse is true.   It is often possible to
irrigate land, but much more difficult to drain it, although it is important to distinguish between land which is wet because of the high precipitation/evaporation
ratio, and land which is wet for other reasons (for instance because of lateral flow
or impermeability of sub-soil).   Again, forests can be planted on first class agricultural land, but they can also be planted, as is now realised, in parts of the West
Highlands, where the soil moisture position is quite unsuitable for agriculture.
The planting of the forests has other effects, as Dr. Calder and Dr. Newson comment
in Chapter 5.   One effect, which they do not touch upon, is that forest cover can
raise the soil temperature by about 1.5°C in winter, and lower it by about 3°C in
summer.

A third, rather more specific point, relates to agricultural drainage.   Dr. Francis
has referred to the climatic constraints affecting *accessibility* to land for agricultural work.   Where land in its natural state is frequently too wet for this,
under-drainage needs to be very efficient.   Tile drains need to be supplemented by
moling or sub-soiling.   In fact, most such *secondary treatment* has been carried out
in the south and east of Britain, not because it is most needed there, but because
the number of days in the year when it can readily be carried out is greatest there,
as is shown in an interesting map prepared by the Field Drainage Experimental Unit.
By comparison, very little secondary treatment has been carried out in Scotland.
That the importance of this treatment is now beginning to be appreciated is shown by
the very recent gradual spread of secondary treatment to north and west Britain.   A
related point is that temporal variation in climate plays a part here.   The excep-
tional run of dry summers recently experienced in eastern Scotland has made under-

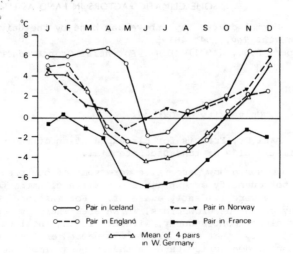

Fig. 4.2 Altitudinal Gradient of Air Temperature Minus Altitudinal Gradient of Soil
Temperature, in Degrees C. per Kilometre (each point on the graphs is the
product of paired observations at particular stations).

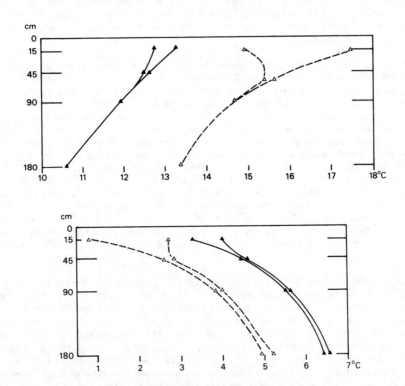

Fig. 4.3 Soil Temperature Observations in Thetford Forest: Top, 3 Aug. 1972:
Bottom, 28 Feb. 1973.   Full line, under woodland: dashed line, under grass
in large clearing (data by courtesy of Institute of Hydrology).
Lowest and highest readings shown at each depth.

drainage seem less necessary to farmers there, and they may be caught out by an ensuing run of wet years.

My fourth comment concerns the rather neglected subject of soil temperatures, on
which Dr. Harding and I have recently been doing some work.   These of course decrease with altitude, but during the growing season this altitudinal decrease is
greater than that of air temperature (Fig. 4.2).   The effects of altitude are much
greater than those of soil type and soil state, but the nature of the surface (vegetation cover, snow cover and aspect for example) is much more important.   I have
mentioned an effect which is under man's control - forest planting (Fig. 4.3), but
snow cover is not.   A continuous winter snow cover, as on the Norwegian fells, pre-
vents soil temperature from falling much below freezing point (Fig. 4.4).   This is
not so on the Scottish hills, where lack of continuous snow protection allows much
more heat to be lost from the soil in winter.

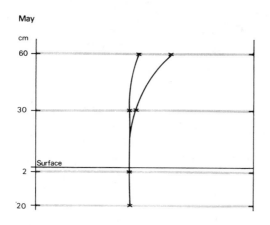

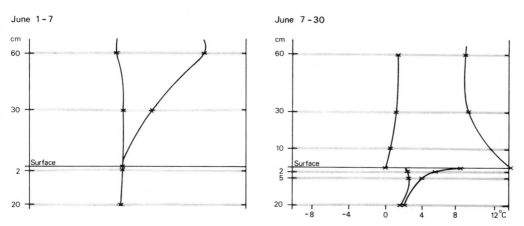

Fig. 4.4 Maximum and Minimum Temperatures at Different Heights,
Stigstuva, 1972.   (Hardangervidda, Norway).
(data by courtesy of A. Skartveit)

These are all additional points, but what Dr. Francis has demonstrated to us is how
some older simplistic parameters need re-examination, and are now receiving it with
the aid of modern facilities.

CHAPTER 5
THE EFFECTS OF AFFORESTATION ON WATER RESOURCES IN SCOTLAND

I.R. Calder and M.D. Newson
Institute of Hydrology

ABSTRACT

The Forestry Commission aims to acquire and plant large areas of upland Britain with conifers, especially in Scotland.   Recent research findings indicate that in the uplands forests are likely to reduce water yields and a simple model, based on these findings, is used to predict the magnitude of this reduction in Scotland.   Typically a decrease of runoff of approximately 20 per cent is predicted as a result of afforestation;   whilst this reduction may not be serious in terms of Scotland's generally abundant resources for water supply there are likely to be operational problems and also more direct disadvantages to other interests, including for example, the generation of hydroelectric power and canal regulation.   There is a need for case studies as afforestation proceeds and for further research into the predictive model and into the other effects of land-use changes on river systems.

KEYWORDS

Reduced water yields;   afforestation;   decrease in runoff;   predictive model;
Scottish uplands.

INTRODUCTION

This topic sits somewhat uneasily at this symposium amongst contributions which investigate the capability of land to sustain a single resource such as forestry or natural habitats.   We, instead, try to detect the influence of a primary use of land, forestry, on a secondary product, water.   We restrict our treatment to the most dynamically-changing type of forestry - coniferous afforestation of the uplands.

Scotland is not short of water resources.   The report published by the Scottish Development Department in 1973 and entitled *A Measure of Plenty* suggested that the 100-fold excess of supply over demand represented a *situation which cannot be described in broad terms as other than satisfactory* (p.5).   The fact that half Scotland lies above 200 m A.O.D. ensures a high average rainfull (1400 mm) and low average rates of evaporative loss (350 mm).   In contrast, England and Wales average only 900 mm of rainfall but 440 mm of loss.   However, the high rainfall and low rates of evaporation from normal crops in Scotland mean that the hydrological effects of afforestation are potentially greater in Scotland than in England and Wales. This is because the higher interception losses from forests in high rainfall areas lead to a much higher annual evaporation compared with that from shorter crops. Since surface impoundments of water in the uplands are likely to be most affected by afforestation, the position in Scotland, where most supplies for domestic and industrial purposes are from such sources, is all the more serious.

Despite the sanguine conclusions of the Scottish Development Department about *broad term* sufficiency of resources, it does admit that shortages occur and will occur more often, as demand grows.   Water is plentiful only if it is available where it is needed and at the time it is needed.   As the report states (p.10) *Water supply schemes have to be designed on the basis of certain assumptions about the amount and distribution of rainfall and about losses by evaporation and transpiration over a period of years*.   Clearly, the biggest threat to such assumptions is climatic variability, i.e., the extremes of flood and drought, but the emphasis here is on a threat which concerns the proportion of rainfall *lost* from the catchment area by evaporation and transpiration.   The implications of increasing losses by afforestation are threefold:

a. The afforestation of existing catchments feeding reservoirs may well reduce the *annual yield* of such reservoirs, and where this yield is highly committed (e.g., for domestic or industrial supply or for making up seepage and operational losses from canals), the scheme may need augmentation.

b. Afforestation also alters the seasonal distribution of runoff which may lead to problems in operating reservoirs by a set of established seasonal rules.   Such *operational problems* apply particularly to schemes for river regulation and power generation;   15 per cent of runoff in Scotland is used for power generation.

c. *Reduction in runoff* in catchments without reservoirs may restrict the choice of sites for future reservoirs.   There are also numbers of regional and local supplies from river intakes in Scotland which will be affected.   The effects on floods, fisheries, recreation and navigation need further investigation in such *natural* catchments.

THE FUTURE RATE OF AFFORESTATION IN SCOTLAND

The biggest potential confrontation between forestry and water collection is where a land-use change (to trees) occurs in the catchment areas where capital investments on water storage have already been made;   these investments may range in cost from those necessary to supply individual farms and hamlets to those required for the installation of large hydro-electric schemes.   Table 5.1 shows that this is very much a *potential* confrontation since present-day levels of afforestation in catchments are low.

If recently-published proposals are implemented, Scotland will experience a large increase of its present forest area by early next century.   Nearly 75 per cent of Scotland is land of the lowest agricultural potential (Agriculture E.D.C., 1977); 62 per cent of the agricultural land is used for rough grazing, compared with less than 30 per cent in Wales and less than 10 per cent in England.   There is a strategic and economic need to lessen the United Kingdom's present level of dependence on imports of timber (92%) and afforestation of a further 3 million ha is required, to double resources of home grown timber by next century (Forestry Commission, 1977, Centre for Agricultural Strategy (in press)).   The lion's share (70%) of the new planting is likely to be in Scotland (Fig. 6.1) and will consequently raise the proportion of reservoirs with significant forest cover in their catchments.   The likely hydrological impact is discussed below.

TABLE 5.1 : Large Reservoirs in Scotland Classified by the Proportion
of Catchment Area Afforested at Present

% forest cover	number of reservoirs
None or very small	22
1 - 10	15
11 - 20	1
21 - 30	1
31 - 40	-
41 - 50	1
>50	-

Source: Ordnance Survey 1:250,000 map

ESTIMATION OF THE IMPACT OF AFFORESTATION ON EVAPORATION AND RUNOFF

Until quite recently, it had been widely believed that the evaporation (made up of both transpiration and interception) from vegetation is *tightly* controlled by the input of solar radiation and hence that the evaporation from all crops (if adequately supplied with water and subject to the same climate) would be broadly similar. Research within the last ten years has, however, shown that this is not necessarily true and, especially in the case of forests, that the energy demands of latent heat for evaporation can even exceed the supply of net solar radiation.   The extra energy is derived from advection, the cooling of the air mass above and within the forest.   Studies of processes and experiments undertaken on catchments by the Institute of Hydrology have shown that massive advection of energy can occur into medium scale forests on a routine basis.   For example, at Plynlimon, Central Wales, the latent-heat demand required to support the annual evaporation from the Hafren forest is found to exceed the annual net radiation input by 12 per cent (Institute of Hydrology, 1976).

Forests are more able to make better use of advected energy than shorter crops be-cause they generate a more turbulent wind regime above their canopies;   this offers less resistance to the transfer of heat and water vapour between vegetative surfaces and the atmosphere.   In wet conditions, during and immediately following rain, the exploitation of this energy source by forests is so efficient that rates of evapor-ation of intercepted water can be as much as ten times those from grass.   This en-hanced rate of evaporation from forests in wet conditions is the principal cause of the extra losses by evaporation that are observed from forests in upland areas com-pared with grassland.

Sophisticated evaporation models have been developed and applied to estimate losses from forests (see, e.g., Calder, 1977, Calder, 1978);   they require a detailed know-ledge both of the prevailing meteorological conditions and of the resistances to the transfer of water within trees and from tree surfaces into the atmosphere.   Unfor-tunately, lack of the detailed data that these models require limits their general applicability at present.   As an interim measure the authors have suggested a more empirical, *broad brush* model which requires only a minimum of readily-available data (Calder and Newson, 1980).   The model is based on the following observations:

(1) Interception losses, expressed as a fraction of the annual precipitation are similar throughout the British uplands (~30%), although reducing slightly with in-creasing rainfall (Fig. 5.1).

(2) The Penman E_t estimate (Penman, 1948), applied on an annual basis, provides a good estimate of the total losses by evaporation from short crops (transpiration

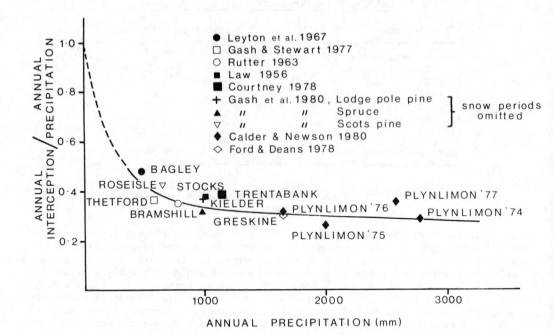

Fig. 5.1 Measurements of Annual Loss by Interception expressed
as a Fraction of the Annual Precipitation Plotted
against Annual Precipitation.

plus interception losses).

(3) Results from a forest lysimeter experiment at Plynlimon suggest that during periods when the canopy is dry, Penman's E_t estimate also provides an approximate estimate of *transpiration* from spruce forest.

(4) Transpiration does not occur whilst forest canopies are wet.

These observations suggest the equation:

Annual evaporation = E_t + f(P x α - w x E_t)

where f = fraction of catchment area covered by a complete canopy,
   P = annual precipitation (mm).
   α = interception fraction, i.e., the fraction of annual precipitation lost to
       interception (determined from Fig. 5.1),
   w = fraction of year when canopy is wet (and no transpiration is taking place).

The effects of afforestation on evaporation loss has been calculated by means of this
model for the catchments which feed the major Scottish reservoirs, i.e., those with
capacities greater than 10 million m³ (Fig. 5.2). Expressed as a reduction in runoff, these figures represent decreases in the range of 15-20 per cent but corres-
pondingly larger decreases in yield (*yield* being the water engineers' unit describing
that portion of runoff which is supplied from a reservoir). A change from grass
vegetation to a forest covering 75 per cent of the area of the catchment is assumed;
this is thought to represent a typical maximum value of afforestation on a Scottish

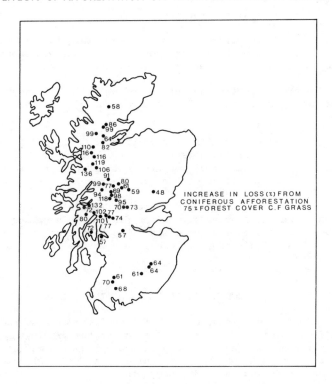

INCREASE IN LOSS(%)FROM
CONIFEROUS AFFORESTATION
75% FOREST COVER C.F GRASS

Fig. 5.2 Predicted Percentage Increase in Loss from Afforesting
(to 75% forest cover) the Catchments Supplying the
Major Scottish Reservoirs

catchment, as the remaining 25 per cent of the land in the catchment area is probably
unsuitable for planting.   The estimates could obviously be improved if information
were available on the proportions of the catchments which are suitable for afforestation.

LIMITATIONS OF THE MODEL

The model is intended to predict, in gross terms, the extra annual evaporation (or
reduction in runoff) which results from afforestation of previously grass covered
regions of the Scottish uplands or other areas of high rainfall in the British Isles.
No claims are made concerning the more general applicability of this simple model on,
for example:

(a) a time scale less than one year;   for instance, during a seasonal drought;
or
(b) conditions in the drier lowland area of the country.

Further caveats must be made concerning the application of the model in situations
in which:

(c) snow assumes a major proportion of the annual precipitation, since the interception component of the model has been developed, in the main, from observations of
differences in *rainfall* above and below forest canopies and it is thought that the
model may well overestimate differences in losses from evaporation between forest

and grassland during years with large snowfalls);
or
(d) the catchment, prior to afforestation, contains large areas under vegetation of
medium height, e.g., bracken, heather or gorse.   In these circumstances, prediction
by the model may again overestimate the effects of afforestation.

Whilst (a) and (b) are currently the subject of general investigation, both (c) and
(d) require further specific research in the context of Scottish climate and land
use.

Meanwhile, for the immediate use of resource planners, the model is believed to give
the best assessment of the likely effects on water supplies.   The model is also
supported by an increasing number of reported case studies sufficient to confirm the
general trend if not the magnitude of the model's predictions.

Furthermore, the predictions of the model are not thought to be particularly sensitive to differences in the species of conifer planted: in upland areas of high rainfall losses from interception are the dominant mechanism of loss and there is no evidence to suggest that significant differences in losses from interception occur between different species of conifers.

THE OPPORTUNITY FOR RESOURCE PLANNING IN SCOTLAND

This paper has attempted to expose a potential conflict of resources and provide an
initial quantification of the effects.   To suggest the likely importance of careful
planning of resource development in the Scottish uplands, a map study was conducted
along similar lines to that undertaken by the Central Water Planning Unit in England
and Wales (Centre for Agricultural Strategy, in press):   a map of catchments was
superimposed on one of the areas suitable for afforestation (Fig. 5.3).   Measurement
by planimeter gave the following proportions of the potentially forested area
(2,217,000 ha) falling within catchments already developed for water collection.
Of the potentially afforestable land in Scotland 24 per cent falls within the catchments of hydro-electric stations;   6 per cent falls within catchments of impounding
reservoirs;   and 10 per cent falls within catchments feeding river intakes.

The study in England and Wales suggested that the first and second categories represented a *serious* effect on water resources with the third, *minor*.   Whilst hydro-
electric generation is not a widespread use of water in England and Wales and is not
treated separately, there are indications (Aitken, 1963) that any reduction of runoff to a power scheme would be serious.   In England and Wales the respective proportions of afforestable land in the *serious* and *minor* categories are 43 and 8 per cent
respectively.

In addition to the evidence of a developing set of case studies involving local re-
ductions of runoff in Scotland, the map study suggests that the impact of further
afforestation may be felt in large catchments also;   the proportion of forest in the
Loch Shin catchment, for example, could rise from 26 to 74 per cent and that in the
Loch Lomond catchment from 11 to 84 per cent.

Although such quantifications are *broad brush* and may suggest an ensuing struggle
between foresters and water engineers, they are intended more as a guide to optimal
upland land use.   The capital costs of replacing sources of water supply have been
given as £100,000 for a decrease in yield of 100 m^3 per day.   Since the decrease
in yields as a result of afforestation can be predicted, it is now possible for econ-
omists to decide how far these costs can be balanced by savings brought about by
reducing imports of timber.

Land suitable for afforestation on major catchments

Land unsuitable for afforestation on major catchments

▲ Local water supply schemes likely to suffer loss of yield from afforestation

0   100km

Fig. 5.3 Major Scottish Catchments Showing Areas Suitable
for Afforestation after G.M.L. Locke.

REFERENCES

Aitken, P.L., (1963). Hydroelectric power generation in *Conservation of Water Resources in the United Kingdom,* Institution of Civil Engineers, 34-42.
Agriculture E.D.C., (1977). *Agriculture into the 80s,* National Economic Development Office, London.
Calder, I.R., (1976). The measurement of water losses from a forested area using a *natural* lysimeter. *J. Hydrol.* 30, 311-325.
Calder, I.R., (1977). A model of transpiration and interceptions loss from a spruce forest in Plynlimon, Central Wales, *J. Hydrol.* 33, 247-265.
Calder, I.R., (1978). Transpiration observations from a spruce forest and comparisons with predictions from an evaporation model, *J. Hydrol.* 38, 33-47.
Calder, I.R. and Newson, M.D., (1980). Land-use and upland water resources in Britain a strategic look, *Water Resources Bulletin,* in press.
Centre for Agricultural Strategy, (1976). *Land for Agriculture,* Reading.
Centre for Agricultural Strategy, (in press). *A Forest Strategy for the UK,* Reading.
Courtney, F.M., (1978). Personal communication.
Ford, E.D. and Deans, J.D., (1978). The effects of canopy structure, stem flow, throughfall and interception loss in a young Sitka spruce plantation, *Jnl. Appl. Ecol.* 15, 905-17.
Gash, J.H.C. and Stewart, J.B., (1977). The evaporation from Thetford Forest during 1975, *J. Hydrol.* 35, 385-96.
Gash, J.H.C., Wright, I.R. and Lloyd, C.R., (1980). Comparative estimates of interception loss from some coniferous forests in Great Britain, submitted to *J. Hydrol.*
Institute of Hydrology, (1976). *Water Balance of the Headwater Catchments of the Wye and Severn, 1970-1974,* Report No. 33.
Law, F., (1956). The effect of afforestation upon the yield of water catchment areas, *Jnl. Br. Waterworks Assn.,* 38, 484-94.
Leyton, L., Reynolds, E.R.C. and Thompson, R.B., (1967). Rainfall interception in forest and moorland, in W.E. Sopper and H.W. Lull (Eds), *Int. Symp. on Forest Hydrology,* Pergamon, Oxford, 163-78.
Rutter, A.J., (1963). Studies in the water relations of *Pinus sylvestris* in plantation conditions. I Measurement of rainfall and interception, *Jour. Ecol.* 51, 191-203.

DISCUSSION

Comment by W.E.S. Mutch, University of Edinburgh.

I regard it as unfortunate that the topic and its treatment invite newspaper feature writers to argue ahead of the facts and to read more into this paper than the authors have written, without *spoiling the story* by repeating the authors' careful caveats. I regret that the paper contains references to *confrontation* and *the ensuing struggle between foresters and water engineers.* Rather than envisaging exclusive use of land we might look for optional combinations of use for society's benefit.

For discussion purposes I wish to raise three matters.

1. Early in the paper there is a reference to the *extra evaporation losses that are observed from forests in upland areas* "compared with grassland". The work on the water interception and use by forests is known and referenced, but I want to enquire about the observations of evaporation/transpiration from grassland, with which the forest results are compared?

Have studies been made on hill grassland which are comparable with the forest studies, on Nardus, Molinia, Deschampsia, or on Trichophorum and Eriophorum? Where are the data derived which have been put into the formula and model? The assertions of Fig. 5.2 depend entirely on these data and it is particularly important to know their provenance and reliability because Calder and Newson deal exclusively with percentage differences and never give the actual figures of interception and use.

The text contains the important caveat that the catchment may contain large areas of bracken and heather, thereby causing the model and the paper to exaggerate the effects of afforestation. I believe there is so much more heather than ryegrass sward in Scottish catchments that the results in Fig. 5.2 given with impressive precision, are probably considerably exaggerated.

2. The authors refer to the effects of afforestation on hydro-electric power generation as being important. I suggest the broad brush treatment is inappropriate in this respect and that each power scheme catchment would require individual consideration.

My knowledge of one catchment at least suggests that a very high proportion of the catchment area, clearly defined by the stream intakes and contour aqueduct, lies above the afforestation level. When allowance is then made for the higher rate of precipitation per unit area on the mountain tops and for the fact that some areas there are bare rock, it seems that the influence of afforestation may be less than the authors suggest. I am not referring to the elevation of the power-stations themselves, for much of the water is used in more than one turbine, but to the proportion of the total water flow which is beyond the influence of afforestation.

The reference to canals is surely not at all important in Scotland. As a first approximation, there seems to be sufficient precipitation falling on the surface of the Caledonian Canal itself (remembering that most of it is between 1 and 2 km wide) to support all its lock operations. It seems highly unlikely that Nessie will find herself short of water as a result of the fullest afforestation imaginable.

3. I want to take up the references to the capital cost of providing additional water supply sources, given as £100,000 for a decrease in water yield of 1000 m^3 per day. The authors' assertions and assumptions in the modelling deserve full investigation before operational decisions are taken, but let us accept for argument that there is a loss of water yield of 420 mm in a precipitation of 2200 mm.

This loss represents 0.42 m^3 per m^2 of forested catchment, that is to say 4200 m^3 per ha per annum loss or 11.7 m^3 per ha per day loss. At this rate 87 ha of afforestation would be required to cause a loss of 1000 m^3 per day, the replacement of which would cost £100,000.

The value of the timber production in terms of import substitution may also be calculated. I use the mean sustained yield of timber in Scotland, 10 m^3 per ha per annum, and the mean value per cubic metre of roundwood equivalent for our current imports. At these rates the value of wood production foregone by denying afforestation is £61,000 per annum; at 5 per cent capitalisation (which is reasonable for long-term investments in water or forestry), this would represent a capital value of £1.2 million.

In this whole topic there is urgent need for more hard data, particularly on the water regime of upland grass and heathland associations, which are crucial to the comparisons and discovery of the optimum mix of land uses to serve society.

Comment by G. Reynolds, North of Scotland Hydro-Electric Board.

I must first declare a vested interest in this topic as I am with the North of Scotland Hydro-Electric Board. The record should be put straight following Dr. Mutch's remarks that the majority of hydroelectric development catchments were above the upper limit of timber growth. The catchment to the lower power stations in Glen Strathfarrar (mentioned specifically by Dr. Mutch) comes down to 40 metres OD, so does the

Loch Awe catchment to Inverawe.   In the extreme west, the Loch Morar catchment falls as low as 10 metres OD but this is an exception.

The figures quoted by Mutch for the value of mean sustained timber yield make no allowances for the maintenance and administrative costs to produce this yield.   It is the nett profit from the timber which has to be compared with the benefits of other forms of land use.   It is my contention that forestry profits come nowhere near balancing the financial value of the water losses when the catchment is afforested, whether the catchment is used for public water supply or hydro-electric development.   Even agricultural or fishery interests could become critically affected in some circumstances.

Finally all energy losses due to reduced water being available following afforestation will need to be replaced from non-renewable sources such as coal or oil.   Is this what the community wants?

Reply by I.R. Calder and M.D. Newson.

In reply to Dr. Mutch's comment about the vocabulary of our paper and the likelihood of its misinterpretation by the Press we would like to emphasise that it is not the intention of the Institute of Hydrology to join a lobby against further afforestation. The use of words like *confrontation* arose from our experience during recent debates and the nature of our presentation here today was deliberately chosen to make impact for our scientific findings of ten years in the pitifully short time of fifteen minutes!   We would, indeed, like to warn the Press to report our work with care and to join Dr. Mutch in a call for further research, especially prior to any detailed use of our extrapolations for Scotland.

We are surprised that, after several years during which discussants have doubted our figures for forest evaporative losses, Dr. Mutch asks for more details of grassland losses.   The use of Penman's E_t for estimating losses from grass-covered catchments (especially catchments in the wetter parts of the country not frequently subjected to high soil moisture deficits) has been largely vindicated over the years by results gathered by the water industry.   Refinements are needed over periods shorter than one year but for annual average values we believe Penman estimates to be reasonable; at Plynlimon estimated and actual average losses for the Wye (grassland) catchment are identical at 425 mm.   Plynlimon has a mixture of all the upland grasses mentioned by Dr. Mutch and by Professor Jarvis.   However, we would fully support their suggestion for further attention to be paid to losses from medium height crops such as *Calluna* and possibly *Pteridium* and also into seasonal losses.   Indeed the Institute of Hydrology is currently making evaporation measurements on these crops in Scotland and the North of England.

With reference to Dr. Mutch's comments on the effects of afforestation on hydro-electric power generation we do not feel able to add to the remarks of Mr. G. Reynolds, included in this Discussion.   Mr. Reynolds has already confirmed the applicability of Penman's estimated losses for a small grassland catchment, part of the Loch Sloy scheme.

The effects of afforestation on water supplies to canals is important in Scotland. We are at present receiving an increasing number of queries from public bodies, water authorities and consulting engineers concerning the effects of afforestation on water supplies and also from the British Waterways Boards who are apprehensive about the effects of the recent afforestation of the catchments which feed the Crinan Canal reservoirs.   The Institute is carrying out a collaborative project with British Waterways Board to investigate this topic.

We cannot join in economic arguments over land use with any conviction since the long-term benefits of any land-use strategy are tied up with the chosen discount rates and these are set by society as a whole.   We have merely repeated in the paper the costs of replacing storage capacity quoted to us by the water industry in England and Wales.

Comment by P.G. Jarvis, University of Edinburgh.

The authors were careful to state that their model and the conclusions from it apply only in the wet, western upland areas of the country. I would like to reiterate this and emphasise the considerable areas of ignorance we face at present in trying to extrapolate their arguments to the drier more eastern parts of the country. There are two points to consider:

a) the instantaneous rates of loss, and
b) the integrated amount of water lost over a period of time.

Generalised values for the instantaneous rates of loss from coniferous canopies are:

| | rates of loss from | | ratio |
| | conifers | grassland | conifers : grass |
		mm/ha	
canopy wet (E_I)	0.3	0.1	3
canopy dry (E_T)	0.15	0.45?	1/3

When the canopy is wet, conifers use about 3 times (not in my view 10 x) as much water as grassland or heathland. However, when the canopy is dry, the rate of evaporation of transpired water from trees may be only 1/3 of that from grassland or heathland. I must emphasise, however, that we know very little about the rates of evaporation from dry canopies of grassland and heathland - far less than we now know about evaporation from conifers - simply because very few reliable measurements have ever been made. I suggest that an estimate based on Penman for evaporation from grassland, applicable at Rothamsted, is totally inappropriate to the kind of vegetation (Calluna, Molinia, Nardus, etc.) found on the hill in upland Scotland. We should now be making a bigger effort to get estimates of evaporation rate and surface resistance of the different kinds of vegetation which are alternatives to forest, including improved agricultural pasture.

Secondly, as one moves east it is also essential to consider the proportion of time that the forest canopy is wet, i.e., the amount of time water loss is at the rate E_I or at the rate E_T. Whereas in the west the forest canopy may be wet with intercepted water for up to 50 per cent of the time, in the eastern side of the country the figure may be less than 10 per cent so that the total loss is dominated by E_T rather than E_I. We have almost no firm information on the proportion of time canopies are wet in different parts of the country. When loss is dominated by E_T rather than E_I, the total loss from coniferous forest will not exceed that from grassland or heathland and may possibly be less.

REFERENCE

Jarvis, P.G. and J. Stewart, (1979) Evaporation of water from plantation forest, In D. Ford and F.T. Last (Eds), *Ecology of Even-aged Plantation*, Proc. IVFRO Div. 1, Edinburgh Univ. Press.

Reply by I.R. Calder and M.D. Newson.

We would like to thank Professor Jarvis for restating the important caveat that our *generalised* evaporation model is only applicable in the wetter upland areas of the country, that is the areas where interception is the dominant loss mechanism.

In the drier lowland areas, where interception is not dominant, we would agree that it is difficult (and may even be misleading) to make any simple generalisations concerning the relative evaporation losses from forest and grassland, except to say that, if differences do exist, they are likely to be very much smaller than those in the wetter parts of the country.   In the lowlands limitations on the availability of soil water are likely to exert a more profound effect upon evaporation rates and it will therefore be necessary to consider at each site of interest the additional variables of soil type, rooting depth and the stomatal response of the crop to soil moisture stress.

When making generalisations confusion may easily arise if the distinction between extreme, instantaneous and long-term average values is not clearly made: in our paper it was stated, as a means of demonstrating the importance of the interception mechanism, that evaporation rates of intercepted water from forests can be as much as 10 x those from grass (i.e., an extreme value), the long-term average value would of course be much less than this.   Similarly we suggest that the value you quote of 1/3 for the ratio of the rates of transpiration from trees and grass may well be applicable to instantaneous rates observed on, for example, a hot summer day with high vapour pressure deficits (limiting forest transpiration) and low soil moisture deficits (encouraging grass transpiration) but would not be representative of the long-term average value which we believe to be much closer to unity.   For example, a ratio of 1/3 for the long-term average at Plymlimon where forest annual transpiration is about 350 mm would indicate a grassland transpiration of more than 1000 mm per year which is in fact more than *twice* that of the observed *total* grassland evaporation (i.e., transpiration and interception).

We would, however, certainly agree that in upland areas transpiration from forests is likely to be rather less than that from grass, and in the model there is to some extent an implicit correction for this in the term WXE_t (This is because E_t on rain days is likely to be less than the mean E_t for wet and dry days).   This justification of the model is however largely unnecessary as we do not pretend that the model predictions are accurate to this degree.   In broad terms we believe the model results to be realistic and as a consequence that in the wetter upland parts of the country trees will on an annual basis always evaporate more water than shorter vegetation.

We thank all three contributors to a lively discussion and apologise to the audience and to other authors for the fact that our topic has demanded so much of the available time.

CHAPTER 6
LAND ASSESSMENT FOR FORESTS

G.M.L. Locke
Forestry Commission

ABSTRACT

The past 30 years has seen a marked increase in the area of woodland in Scotland,
almost entirely by extension onto rough grazings that have not borne trees within
living memory.   Land being considered for acquisition is mapped to show soil and
vegetation and plantable areas defined which are then subdivided into zones to
which growth rates, rotations, fertiliser requirements, costs of establishment and
maintenance and revenues can be attributed; the assessment is both detailed and
ad hoc.   To assess total plantable land; an evaluation was made at the 1:625,000
scale of rough grazing, mainly on the basis of elevation and exposure, to identify
areas likely to produce satisfactory growth rates.   The resulting maps were then
amended after comment by local staff; the approach worked well except in North
Scotland, where alternative local sources were used.   The results yield an estimate
of 1.7 million ha of land capable of growing economic crops of timber.

KEYWORDS

Afforestation in Scotland; rough grazings; land acquisition; growth rates;
exposure; plantable land.

The last 30 years have seen a very marked increase in the area of woodland in Scotland.   It has risen from about 500,000 ha in 1947 to the current figure of about
865,000 ha.   Part of this increase is due to the work of the Forestry Commission
and part to that of individual private owners or forestry groups.   All the increase,
however, has been as a result of extension of forest on to land which has not borne
trees within living memory and, in almost all cases, on to land classified as rough
grazing.

When land is considered for acquisition for forestry the process in the Forestry
Commission follows a fairly general pattern and it is expected that other buyers of
land for forestry will use a similar approach.   First, the land has to come on the
market and the size of the area, its shape and whether the sale involves buildings
as well as land, will differ from case to case.   If part or all of the area is
suitable for afforestation the block will then be inspected and the land classified
and mapped according to major soil types and vegetational complexes.   The proportion
which is considered suitable for forestry is then defined.   This plantable area is
sub-divided on the basis of soil groups and elevational zones into categories to

which can be attributed growth rates for the major species, the likely rotations, the expected fertiliser regime, the likely cost of establishment and maintenance, and the expected revenues.   This approach enables the prospective purchaser to calculate what is the maximum price he can afford to pay for the land so as to give him a set return on the whole investment before he makes his bid.   The essential part of this procedure, however, is that the land is examined in detail, decisions are made on the ground as to what is plantable and what is not.   Small variations in land form which can affect the degree of exposure can be taken into consideration and all these boundaries are capable of being mapped.   The areas of plantable land which emerge from this examination are therefore objective and reasonably accurate, and the boundaries have been drawn using knowledge of the current capability of machinery and current forest practice.   The upper plantable limit will have been set at a level that will result in the production of utilisable crops of timber up to this level, although the term *plantable limit* does not have a fixed or formal definition and will differ from place to place, from time to time, and indeed, to some degree, from individual to individual.

ASSESSING THE PLANTABLE AREA

When the question was raised, therefore, of how much land there is in Scotland which is technically plantable, i.e., capable of growing utilisable crops of trees, it posed a number of problems.   First, there is the problem of how to make an estimate of a category that essentially needs inspection on the ground to make a practical assessment.   The second problem is how to define the term *technically plantable*, which is a judgment that must vary with individual circumstances and is therefore difficult to apply on a national scale.   The third problem is how to obtain an estimate of plantable land when there is at present a very real lack of knowledge about soil in the uplands.   Until now most of the work of the Macaulay Institute has rightly been devoted to the lowland soils.   It has been largely left to foresters to map the upland soils in those areas where they have acquired land for the growing of trees.   The nature and depth of soil are crucial in determining which species can be grown and which not, at what rates they will grow, to what rotation lengths and whether they can be thinned.   All these factors are critical in deciding whether an investment in forestry is going to be viable or not.   Lastly, there is the problem of how to get a broad estimate of what is plantable when local land forms are so important.   Quite extensive areas of land may be largely unsuited for tree growth because of exposure but within them there could well be blocks, which would naturally be more expensive to establish and maintain, that could still produce productive crops.

The problem was therefore to adopt an approach that would enable an extensive view to be taken of the potential, to map it at a relatively small scale, so that it was not necessary to become involved with detail, but still enable local knowledge and experience to play a part in determining the boundaries and areas.

There are, essentially, three factors which have to be considered in determining whether forestry can be extended on to bare land - topography, soils and climate. At times one of these factors may be limiting on its own account but more usually it is their effect in combination that determines whether the area can be planted or not.

Topography

Topography affects forestry mainly as a result of its influence on soil and climate, which are considered next, but the physical configuration of the ground can have a marked effect on costs of operations such as fencing, ploughing and timber extraction, and difficult terrain inevitably leads to increased costs of operations.

Soil

Increasing elevation usually results in soils becoming shallower and also thinner
and stonier; but, provided there is sufficient soil above bed-rock, modern techniques of forestry ensure that there are now few soils that cannot be drained or
cultivated by ploughing or whose mineral deficiencies cannot be rectified by fer-
tilisation.   The old dictum, however, that the better the soil the better the growth
holds good for trees as well as for arable crops, and soils that require extensive
initial treatment, or whose mineral deficiencies have to be rectified on a regular
and continuing basis, tend to lead to higher costs.

Climate

In general Scotland has a climate which is very favourable for tree growth, but
there is no doubt it is a very windy country and the prevalence of gales leads to
the risk of windthrow and breakage of stems.   The combination of galeforce winds
and unstable soils usually leads to a management decision to lessen the risk by
adopting shorter rotations, possibly with no thinning as well.   Another factor of
climate is temperature.   It is seldom limiting to tree growth by itself but
increasing elevation leads to higher exposure and lower temperatures and these can
quickly become limiting to a more marked degree than in almost any other country in
Western Europe.   This is one of the reasons why the Scottish hills, in spite of
their moderate elevation, are seldom planted with trees above 500 m in the south
and east, above 400 m in the west and 300 m in the north and north-west.   On exposed sites the plantable limit may well be less than 200 m.

With the low ground largely excluded from forestry because of agricultural and
urban use, and the topmost ground excluded because of exposure, low temperatures
and shallow soils, forestry is essentially an industry of the foothills and uplands.
Land for expansion is therefore largely limited by physical factors.

The problem therefore was to try and find a simple method of calculating how much
additional land was capable of being planted with trees after due allowance had
been made for the basic factors of topography, soil and climate and also for the
fact that certain tracts of land have to be excluded because they are urban or
under intensive agricultural management.

THE METHOD ADOPTED

The method adopted was first to obtain guidance as to the location of the major
land type suitable for afforestation, namely heathland, moorland and rough grazing,
and for this purpose, use was made of Dudley Stamp's map of land utilisation at a
scale of 1:625,000, derived from the survey undertaken in the 1930s.   Although the
maps are out of date the broad general pattern is still valid and so formed a
basis on which to work.   The major concentrations of land in these upland categories were therefore transferred to an outline map.   All other agricultural land
classes, viz., those classed as arable, rotational or permanent pasture, were
entirely excluded from further consideration as were urban land, land under roads,
rail and other communications, and forest and woodland already on the map.   Only
major blocks of hill land were further considered.   The next step was to sub-divide
this land into that part which was at lower elevations, and therefore likely to be
plantable, from that at higher elevations where growth is likely to be much slower
and therefore tree crops are less commercially viable.   Elevation itself is not a
particularly good criterion because the plantable limit can differ from place to
place and differ quite markedly.   It was therefore decided to use an index which
did more than just define elevation but also build in other relevant factors.   Use
was therefore made of the work of E.L. Birse and B. Robertson, whose work in
assessing climatic conditions in Scotland is well known, and in particular their

publication showing the mapped boundaries of exposure and accumulated frost.   An
added benefit was that their map was at the same scale as Dudley Stamp's map, which
made the transfer of detail relatively easy.   The boundaries of the climatic types
defined by Birse and Robertson were not always followed precisely but all categories
of extremely exposed and very exposed land were excluded as well as some of the
exposed land, and this naturally removed very substantial areas from further consideration.   Their exclusion does not imply that within these categories there is
no plantable land, but merely that it is unlikely to be present in substantial
quantities.

The result was a map which, in general terms, showed hill land that was not too
exposed for reasonable tree growth and which had effectively an in-built elevational
limit which varied according to location.

Maps showing the estimated areas of potentially plantable land were then sent to
the Forestry Commision's Conservators who in turn discussed the assessments with
local staff.   They were asked if the boundaries shown appeared reasonable and, if
not, to amend them using their own local knowledge.

Their comments showed that, in general, the approach seemed to have worked fairly
well.   Adjustments were made to boundaries but certainly in South, West and East
Scotland the changes were minor and the end result one which local staff were
willing to accept as a reasonable estimate of the forestry potential - always
bearing in mind the limitations of the approach and of the scale at which the assessment was being mapped (Fig. 6.1).   In North Scotland, however, the method, which
had worked fairly satisfactorily over three-quarters of the country resulted in a
very substantial over-estimate.   The factors which caused this over-estimate are
complex but it is thought that two in particular were involved.   First, in the
north there are very substantial areas of shallow soils or where rock outcrops at
the surface and these can very quickly reduce the effective plantable area, and
indeed exclude some areas altogether.   The second is that there are very substantial areas of peat in this conservancy, often with inherently expensive drainage
problems associated with them.   In both instances these are factors which are
difficult enough to map at the best of times, even at a fairly large scale, and the
use of a small scale in this assessment merely aggravated the difficulty.   The end
result, therefore, was that in North Scotland the map had produced merely a first
estimate which was subsequently modified by local staff using local knowledge.
There was, however, no way in which the boundaries on the map could be modified to
reflect this reduced area without an immense amount of work and they were accordingly
left untouched.

There was one other aspect which had to be considered at this stage.   The boundaries
of the rough grazing land as set out on Dudley Stamp's map related basically to the
pre-war situation but it was known that, owing to the spread of years over which the
survey was taken, many of the totals of areas of woodland quoted in that survey were
low and it was suspected that the map would likewise under-represent the presence
of woodland.   Limitations of scale would also prevent the representation of all but
the larger blocks.   Rather than merely deduct the area of woodland which was estimated to have been afforested in the uplands since the war (and the calculation
of this total would have posed quite a problem), it was decided to deduct the total
area of woodland irrespective of its location.   The adoption of this decision is
likely to have produced an underestimate of the area of plantable land, as a good
deal of the woodland is at low elevations and so would have been automatically excluded from the calculations.   However, it is felt that the final estimate of 1.7
million hectares of land suitable for planting which has arisen from this study,
although probably an underestimate, gives a reasonable approximation of the area
which could produce utilisable crops of timber.   The operative word here is could -
not should or will.   It is a figure of potential only.

Potentially
Plantable Land

Forestry Commission Land
and Dedicated and Approved Land

0   50   100 Km

Fig. 6.1 Potentially Plantable Land, Forestry Commission Land
and Dedicated and Approved Land

CONCLUSION

It must also be clear that such an approach is no substitute for ground survey, for this is the only method by which an objective estimate of the area of plantable land can be made.   The approach used here was a means to an end, not an end in itself, and local knowledge played a major part in determining the final estimates.

REFERENCES

Birse, E.L. and B. Robertson, (1970). *Assessment of Climatic Conditions in Scotland 2. Based on exposure and accumulated frost.*, Macaulay Institute for Soil Research, Aberdeen.

Locke, G.M.L., (1976). *The Place of Forestry in Scotland*, Forestry Commission Research and Development Paper 113, Edinburgh.

Stamp, D., (1944). *Land Utilisation Survey of Britain*, 10 miles to one inch maps, Sheets 1 and 2, Ordnance Survey.

CHAPTER 7
ASSESSMENT OF LAND FOR NATURE CONSERVATION

J. McCarthy
Nature Conservancy Council

ABSTRACT

Because nature conservation is not considered a productive use and non-economic judgments are often involved, a policy for nature conservation must take account of many
other rural land uses.   Any assessment for nature conservation must be based on an
understanding of the abundance, distribution and status of habitats and of species.
The selection of sites by the Nature Conservancy Council is based upon type of habitat,
but whilst the scientific description of sites is relatively straightforward, the
evaluation of attributes is not; there is a wide range of value judgments, whether
intrinsic or based upon actual and potential use.   Site selection must also take
account of the feasibility of protection and management.   The aim should be adequate
protection of a representative range of the major ecosystems, with priority to those
species under greatest threat; this is the rationale behind the Nature Conservation
Review.   There is a strong case for taking account, not only of *intrinsic* merit, but
also of the scientific and social needs of the community.

KEYWORDS

Value judgments; site selection; Nature Conservancy Council; Nature Conservation
Review; intrinsic merit; protection and management.

INTRODUCTION

Assessments of land for nature conservation pose a peculiar problem : whereas there
is a generally accepted recognition of the need for land for industrial development,
agriculture and forestry, as uses contributing directly to basic human economic requirements, nature conservation involves a consideration of aesthetic, ethical, scientific and educational values which are difficult, if not impossible, to quantify in
conventional terms.   This is not to under-rate such values which are increasingly
recognised as vital for human health and welfare, but, in the context of other material demands of society, only a limited proportion of land in such a highly-populated
country can be set aside exclusively for this purpose.   Much more frequently, nature
conservation is a subsidiary use, or even a by-product of other traditional land uses,
and any process of assessment must take this into account.   This process involves
identifying the characteristics of any given area, assessing its value in relation to
other comparable areas and, given the limitations already noted, selecting those sites
regarded as most important at national, regional and local levels.   The basic

objective is to ensure the protection of the best viable examples of the country's *natural* and semi-natural habitats with their associated plant and animal populations over the whole range of ecological variation within Scotland, in terms both of their intrinsic features and of their potential use for purposes of nature conservation.

This ecological variation is reflected in the range of climatic, physiographic, edaphic and anthropogenic factors which combine to produce recognisable habitat types (*formations*) such as coast, woodland, upland and open waters, and it is these habitat types and their variants which provide the basis of a classification for ecological assessment : for nature conservation purposes, native plants and animals cannot be isolated from the environment which supports them. Within such a framework, it is possible to compare the features of, for example, different oakwoods or saltmarshes, and to evaluate these against a standard set of quality criteria.

SITE SURVEY

Two distinct processes are involved in site surveys. The first is a factual identification and scientific recording of the attributes of the area concerned which, although time-consuming and often involving a wide range of expertise - in geology, botany, ornithology and the like - is relatively straightforward and can use standard techniques. These include scrutiny of maps, interpretation of aerial photographs, description of main habitats and communities present, lists of species and site factors such as geology, topography and soil types. Many of the more important areas already have considerable background literature and reports, but there is no substitute for detailed field survey by competent ecologists, who must have a wide taxonomic expertise, especially in the identification of plant species. With non-specialist surveyors there is inevitably a tendency to concentrate on the most obvious and easily identifiable features of a site and to overlook more obscure species of, for example, mosses or invertebrates which may constitute the most important values of the site. A further important consideration in field survey is obviously timing : some sites are primarily important for their populations of wintering wildfowl, while others are noted for localised plant species with a very restricted summer flowering season. Ideally a site should be surveyed at different seasons over a number of years to build up a comprehensive picture and to indicate whether populations are stable or ephemeral

So far the word *site* has been used as if the area being assessed was self-defining. In intensively-managed countryside this is frequently the case, since our semi-natural habitats, such as woodland and marsh, have become so fragmented that there is a clear-cut margin between these and adjacent farmland or commercial forest. Over much of upland Scotland, however, this is not the case and there may be considerable difficulties over large tracts of superficially similar country in defining boundaries which encompass the main interest of the site but do not include an excessive area. In the absence of other criteria, practical considerations apply, such as the use of obvious features for demarcation, such as roads and walls, or boundaries of property units.

SITE EVALUATION AND CRITERIA FOR SELECTION

The second process of assessment of value is much more complex because of its subjectivity and the difficulty of quantifying very disparate (and sometimes apparently conflicting) criteria. A detailed rationale for the selection of biological sites of national importance to nature conservation in Great Britain is given by Ratcliffe (1977) and this has now been generally adopted by the Nature Conservancy Council for the assessment of all potentially important sites at regional and local level. A major element in the problem is that assessment is concerned not with absolutes, but with relative values - if there were only one native pinewood in Scotland, there would be no difficulty in selection! On the other hand, it can be claimed with some justification that no two sites are identical in all their attributes, i.e., each site is *unique*, and yet this cannot be said categorically until the total field of variation is known, which is certainly not true of the more remote habitats in certain parts of Scotland.   Conservationists are often accused of over-emphasising rarity as a criterion, but there are very practical reasons for protecting rare species or communities : first, these are often reflections of an unusual combination of site factors which may provide important scientific insights into ecological relationships, and secondly, by definition, they are vulnerable and therefore a priority for protection.   The continuously-updated Atlas of the British Flora (and associated distribution maps for animal groups) fortunately provides a means of assessing the range, frequency and distribution of most plant species and many of the animals in Great Britain.   The rarest of these are listed in the Conservation of Wild Creatures and Wild Plants Act, 1975, and this has also been used as a guide to site selection.

In an intensively-developed country, with most semi-natural habitats broken up into small discrete areas, many sites are analogues to *islands* whose size and spatial relationships with other similar habitats may determine the diversity and survival of species : the minimum size required is now known for certain birds and insects, for example, and the criterion of extent of site is regarded as especially important in comparative evaluation;   there is now general agreement that woodlands, for example, should not be less than 20 ha in extent if they are to be for viable sites.   For uplands, this size criterion is very much more difficult to establish : while certain types of upland vegetation could be represented adequately on 100 ha or less, the full altitudinal range is not usually available over less than 1,000 ha.   The situation becomes very much more complicated if the required feeding ranges of upland birds, for example, are to be included since the territory of a Golden Eagle may be measured in square kilometres, depending on the availability of prey.

This criterion may be associated with another - that of diversity - which is used to distinguish sites which are in other respects comparable.   Site diversity is in turn closely related to differences in topography, local climate and soils which often demonstrate important ecological gradients, with parallel variety in numbers of both communities and species.   In some cases, diversity has been brought about by human intervention and management, for example, peat diggings or the introduction of species. This form of diversification must be weighed against the attribute of *naturalness* which is probably one of the most difficult of criteria to identify in a country where severe modification of habitats has been the rule rather than the exception, and where there can be no certainty as to what the *natural* condition might have been prior to man's intervention through clearance, grazing, burning, drainage, cultivation and the like.   Some indication of the degree of modification can, however, be obtained from the recorded history of a site (which itself can be regarded as a criterion of value), including pollen analytical studies showing the historical development of a habitat over considerable periods of time.

If it is accepted that the aim is to protect examples from the whole field of available ecological variation, it follows that these examples should be typical and representative habitats (in terms of their site features, and plant and animal populations) and in this respect, many sites considered of value by NCC may differ from those selected by other voluntary conservation bodies whose membership may be attracted by more spectacular or unusual situations.   By definition *representativeness* frequently involves an identification of geographical variants reflecting distinctive climatic and geological conditions.   Thus, within the uplands of Scotland it is possible to distinguish a climatic range from south to north of decreasing temperature as represented, for instance, by number of growing days per annum, and a corresponding east-west gradient of increasing oceanicity manifested in wind exposure and number of frost-free days.   Compared with mainland Europe, the mountain systems of Great Britain are noted for this characteristic of oceanicity, and an associated lowering of the altitude of vegetation zones, the latter usually being clearly identifiable. These features of the British uplands are sufficiently rare on a world scale to make the resulting flora and fauna of international importance, especially when they are combined with historical factors of glaciation and subsequent human use.   It is possible in this way to differentiate between the Southern Uplands, the Grampian Mountain system, the North-West Highlands and the northern island groups of Orkney and Shetland, and within these to distinguish representation of particular plant and animal communities and species associated often with distinctive rock and derived soil formations, e.g., serpentine.   It is not surprising, given these considerations that the distribution of important upland sites in Britain is markedly biassed towards Scotland, more particularly the Scottish Highlands, and that the area occupied by important biological sites within this habitat is relatively large (Fig. 7.1).

By contrast, the representation of open waters, including loch and river systems, is based on different parameters, although similar general criteria of selection are used.   In particular, aquatic invertebrate and phytoplankton fauna are used to categorise different types of bodies of open water, in addition to their vascular flora The decisive factor influencing the flora and fauna of standing waters is the chemica content of the water, which largely determines its productivity - for example, phosphate, which limits algal development.   Alkalinity is the most convenient measure of overall chemical content and open-water systems can be distinguished on a scale ranging from extremely nutrient-rich (eutrophic) to very nutrient poor (oligotrophic), and other special categories in which the nutrient status is not directly reflected by calcium content, but by salinity, for instance, or the presence of phosphorus in insoluble form.   Sub-divisions of these main categories are possible using such physical attributes as depth of water, area and nature of shoreline to provide a range of ecological variation within which the best examples can be selected for representation of nature conservation interests.   In this process, the degree of disturbance will be an important additional consideration, especially in relation to populations of breeding and roosting birds.   Although Scotland is favoured in its plentiful loch systems, the majority of these are oligotrophic and the distribution of nationally important examples is again skewed : in this case, much of the range of the eutrophic series is to be found in England, although Loch Leven, near Kinross, is an outstanding example of a classic shallow lowland eutrophic loch which has been the subject of intensive research for many years under the International Biological Programme.

These two examples of representation of major habitat formations, i.e., uplands and open waters, illustrate the complexities involving one criterion alone (typicality) in making assessments of nature conservation value and the level of scientific information required to ensure these are not arbitrary.

ECOLOGICAL CHANGE AND MANAGEMENT POTENTIAL

Traditionally, the assessment of land for nature conservation has been based on the attributes of an area at one point in time, reflected in the emphasis on scientific description and evaluation of observed features.   Although ecologists recognise that all natural systems are dynamic and that change in time and space is inevitable, there is often a reluctance to appreciate the implications of this in assessment, especially in relation to management potential.   These changes in composition, structure, and distribution of plant and animal communities may result from natural factors, such as climatic change, or be man-induced, as with burning and grazing. If areas are selected for particular present attributes to represent examples within the range of ecological variation, it is important to know whether their present condition is a desirable ecological end point, whether this is likely to alter, or indeed whether direct change by positive management is required.

Although there is a strong argument in favour of acquiring nature conservation areas for their long-term protection and to pre-empt threats to their existing scientific interest, there is an equally strong case for placing a priority on those areas which

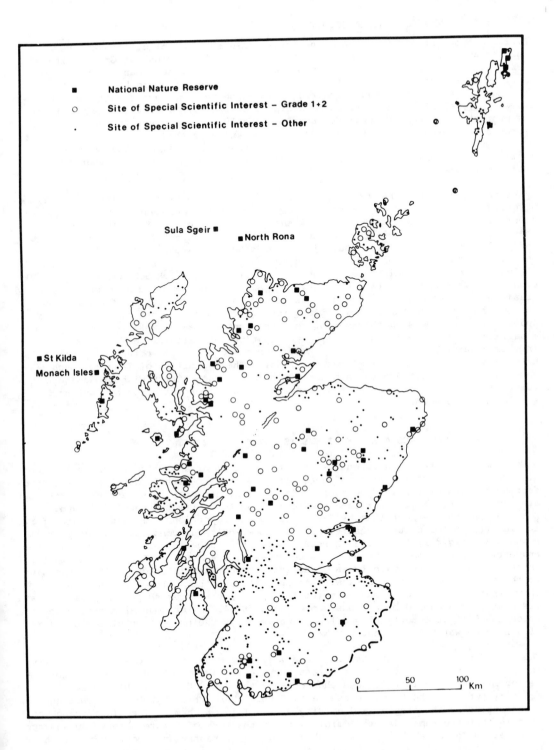

Fig. 7.1 Nature Conservation in Scotland : Statutory Sites

offer the best options for developing their management potential to meet the requirements of a comprehensive policy for nature conservation throughout Great Britain.
Where the area is already in a desirable and stable condition, management may be
directed at maintaining the *status quo* : in other cases it could be aimed at diver-
sifying present habitats and populations (as is being done successfully on Rhum and
elsewhere), rehabilitating degraded habitats, or creating improved conditions for
the protection of species that are rare nationally.   Some areas, because of such
features as their ecological history, land use and ownership and location, are clearly
more suitable than others for one or more of these purposes, and the process of assessment should be extended beyond existing criteria to include this important practical consideration.

Apart from protecting the widest possible range of the nation's wildlife as a desirable object *per se*, the assessment of areas for nature conservation should take account of legitimate associated uses of the sites selected.   The most obvious of
these is research to increase our fundamental understanding of ecological systems
and processes, and to provide facilities for study and experiment.   Closely allied
to this is the educational function, which can range from broadly-based public information services to specific provision for school project work and university field
studies.   Many national nature reserves in Scotland occupy land of high amenity and
traditional recreational areas, and management for public access and maintenance of
landscape, while not the exclusive function of NCC, must pay due regard to this.
Indeed, it could be said that one of the functions of nature reserves is to provide
management experience in such uses, given that the exercise of nature conservation
in this country is largely one of integrating a wide range of potentially competing
uses on a limited area of semi-natural land.   The capability of land for such purposes and its capacity to sustain use at different intensities without damage to
vulnerable features must be part of assessment, both for selection and any necessary
subsequent management.

LAND USE AND AREA REQUIREMENTS FOR NATURE CONSERVATION

Quite apart from the need to ensure that the most important wildlife sites are identified, any organisation which of necessity must resist certain developments to protect such sites is required to justify its claims, not only in scientific terms, but
also in the context of other land uses competing for a limited supply of land.
Notwithstanding the fact that by far the largest proportion of land designated for
its importance for nature conservation is either quite uneconomic to develop or is
classed as *marginal*, fears are expressed about the number of sites involved and the
proportion of any one region which is considered *protected*.   Figure 7.2 indicates
the proportions of the main types of habitat in Scotland in Grade 1 sites according
to the Nature Conservation Review.   An analysis of other sites (Grades 2 and 3)
shows that these proportions are maintained, i.e., that over 48 per cent of the land
designated is occupied by uplands above 1,500 ft (457 m) or coastal areas, much of
which is cliff or intertidal mudflat.   Conversely, the proportion of lowland (excluding open waters) is minute (0.8%).

The second point is illustrated in Table 7.1.   At present, National Nature Reserves
occupy just over 1 per cent of the land surface area of Scotland.   What is not revealed by the table is that less than one-quarter (20,000 ha) of this percentage is
actually owned by the Nature Conservancy Council, and that 10,000 ha of that quarter
are occupied by the single land holding of the Isle of Rhum.   The significance of
this is that the remainder is administered in the form of Nature Reserve Agreements
which allow for other land uses, such as grazing, forestry and sport, often with
minimal constraints on traditional management.   This is true to an even greater
extent for those areas not declared as National Nature Reserves, since the form of
protection usually adopted, i.e., notification as a Site of Special Scientific Interest (under Section 23 of the National Parks and Access to the Countryside Act of

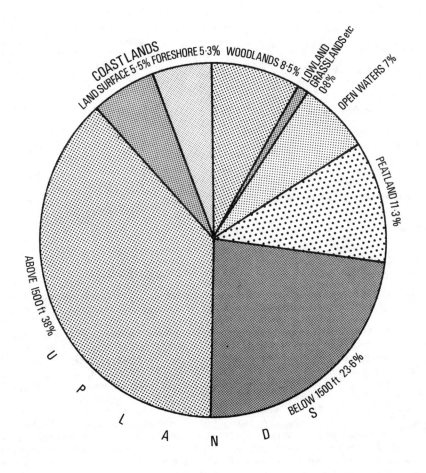

Source: Nature Conservancy Council, (1977). A Nature Conser-
        vation Review: Towards Implementation.   A consul-
        tative paper (unpublished).

Fig. 7.2 Grade 1 Sites in Scotland by Habitat

1949), merely enables consultation to take place with the local planning authority
when development (which excludes agriculture and forestry) is proposed.   The fact
that nature conservation values can often be maintained (and sometimes enhanced) in
conjunction with other forms of land use and management is clearly of relevance to
the process of assessment for nature conservation, but is not always appreciated
when, on the basis of these assessments, notification of new areas is proposed.
Part of the problem is not only that the implications of such notification are mis-
understood, but that certain regions such as the North-West of Scotland have a dis-
proportionate area of land which qualifies for designation : the total area here
rises from the Scottish average of 8.77 to 14 per cent.   When other designations
such as National Park Direction Areas and landscape areas are added, it is not surprising that the authorities concerned, often with an eye to potential inhibitions

TABLE 7.1   Statutory Nature Conservation Sites in Scotland[1]

	No. of Sites	Area (ha)	% Scotland Land Area
National Nature Reserves (NNR)	52	89,270	1.16
[2] Nature Conservation Review (Grade 1 and 2 sites)	199	373,048	4.80
Other Sites of Special Scientific Interest (SSSI)	716	189,577	2.15
TOTALS	967	651,895	8.01

Source: Author, from NCC records.

[1] As at January 1979

[2] Excluding NNR for purposes of calculation

on economic development and prospects for employment in underdeveloped areas, question both the justification and the implications of such evaluations.

The question of the number of sites for nature conservation and their distribution, which has been mentioned earlier under criteria for assessment, raises a number of fundamental issues for nature conservation policy in this country.   The first is whether or not a target should be set for the number of sites, as represented by the total proportion of land by area, which should be protected for purposes of nature conservation.   Theoretically, and given the proposition that each semi-natural area is *unique* (in the sense previously defined), this could be completely open-ended, to embrace all the remaining semi-natural habitats available.   On the basis that in certain parts of Great Britain, development (particularly intensifi-cation of agriculture) has drastically reduced and modified wild communities of plants and animals, this would not seem unreasonable as an insurance policy against the cer-tainty that there will be pressures in future to diminish this biological resource further.   The International Union for the Conservation of Nature has suggested that not less than 5 per cent by area of any one country should be protected as *nature reserves* and by their definition, the figure for Great Britain (and for Scotland) falls well below that (Table 7.1).   If, however, Sites of Special Scientific Interest (SSSI) and other designations are added, it would be possible to achieve this figure, and somewhere between 5 - 10 per cent would be appropriate, given the protective limitations of such designations.   The present figure for Great Britain as a whole is approximately 5.7 per cent.

THE FUTURE

The position in Scotland is somewhat different, insofar as climate and economies have inhibited intensive development of large tracts of countryside and are likely to do so in the foreseeable future.   Two factors can alter this situation quite dramatic-ally : the first could be a change in agricultural policies for hill land in Scotland arising from demands from the European Economic Community (and therefore price levels) for meat animals raised in the uplands.   The second could be a more positive Govern-ment policy in favour of forestry.   A recent paper on forestry prospects in Great

Britain has indicated that a further 1.8 million ha of land have potential for commerical planting, the bulk of this in Scotland, and the forest industry has consistently advocated greater self-sufficiency and less reliance on expensive imports of timber.   Both the agricultural and the forestry lobbies have made specific claims for the proportion of land required for the needs of their respective interests. Both of these are valid economic uses, readily recognised by the community as such, even if their protagonists consider them under-rated in terms of the nation's welfare.

The case for an equivalent claim for nature conservation will largely rest on its perceived benefits to society, not only in general terms of a capital wildlife resource which is as much part of our heritage as historical monuments, but also specifically for such necessary uses as scientific research, education and public amenity. It is clearly not sufficient to secure a restricted sample of our nationally important biological sites within the remaining semi-wilderness areas of the country, since their inaccessibility would severely restrict their use for these purposes. Given that the majority of users live in major centres of population in the lowlands surrounded by highly modified countryside, it is vitally important that there should be a reasonable geographic spread of a wide variety of protected semi-natural habitats, representing both national and local needs, so that nature conservation is recognised and valued as an integral component of the environment in which people work and live.

REFERENCES

Perring, F.H. and S.M. Walters, (Eds)., (1976). *Atlas of the British Flora.*   Bot. Soc. Br. Isl.
Ratcliffe, D.A.R. (Ed)., (1977). *A Nature Conservation Review,* Cambridge University Press, Cambridge.

CHAPTER 8
SCOTLAND'S SCENIC HERITAGE

J.R. Turner
Countryside Commission for Scotland

ABSTRACT

A report in 1978 attempted to identify areas of fine landscape that should be conserved as part of the national heritage.   Existing designated areas were reviewed
together with the results of a preparatory survey.   A desk analysis of the resulting
areas was followed by field survey, using a consistent team of 2-3 surveyors to make
a subjective appraisal.   Results were submitted to a steering group and to the
Countryside Commission for Scotland, and 40 National Scenic Areas identified, concerning 12.7 per cent of the country.   These comprise the areas in which there is
a national interest, and it is hoped they will be valuable to local planning authorities.   A corollary of this approach is the need to develop policies for those areas
that are of regional and local significance.   This appraisal is likely to lead to
new National Planning Guidelines for scenic conservation.

KEYWORDS

Countryside Commission for Scotland; Scotland's Scenic Heritage; National Scenic
Areas; planning for conservation; National Planning Guidelines; subjective
appraisal.

INTRODUCTION

It is one of the apparent inconsequentialities of modern Scotland, a developed
nation with an advanced system of land-use planning, is that there are no national
parks.   In England and Wales there are ten, which come into the category V of the
classification of National Parks and Protected Areas, recently prepared by the
International Union for the Conservation of Nature and Natural Resources.   That
there should be none in Scotland, a country renowned for its scenic beauty, is a
source of surprise to visitors.   The House of Commons Select Committee on Land
Resource Use remarked upon this apparent inconsistency in 1972, and in 1974 the
Countryside Commission for Scotland published a report *A Park System for Scotland*.
This report considered carefully the question of developing national parks in Scotland on the lines adopted in many other countries throughout the world and concluded
that, for a variety of reasons to do with the form of central and local government
organisation and with land-ownership and management, national parks would require a
radical new approach to conservation in Scotland.   It was concluded that the same
objectives of improving opportunities for the enjoyment of the countryside whilst

79

conserving its recreational and scenic attributes could be achieved in other ways.

The Commission's proposals were then divided into two broad parts.   The first related to the making of recreational provisions comprising a system of special parks,
regional parks, country parks and linear and local facilities, and the second to the
development of policies and procedures for the conservation of those areas of country
side of unsurpassed attractiveness which are part of the national heritage, but
which for the most part do not require significant recreational provisions to be
made in them (Fig. 8.1).   The report was accepted by the Secretary of State for
Scotland in March 1976 which meant that two initial requirements needed to be fulfilled.   The Secretary of State indicated that he would seek to have the necessary
legislation enacted to enable a park system to be set up when legislative time could
be found and it was possible to accommodate the proposals within the Government's
programme for public expenditure.   In the expectation that the recreation-related
proposals would thus be implemented, it was also necessary for the Commission to
develop in more detail the outline proposals contained in *A Park System for Scotland*
for the conservation of areas of outstanding scenic interest.   In April 1978 the
Commission published *Scotland's Scenic Heritage,* a review identifying those parts
of Scotland which require this particular kind of care and attention.

EARLIER APPROACHES

The existing arrangements under the Planning Acts to secure the conservation of
scenic interest fall into two categories.   First, there is provision for national
oversight in five areas which were identified in directions issued by the Secretary
of State for Scotland in 1948, and are known as National Park Direction Areas.
These areas were those suggested for designation as national parks in Scotland in
reports submitted by the Scottish National Parks Survey Committee (1945) and the
Scottish National Parks Committee (1947).   These directions were issued to secure
a measure of added planning control in the context of a decision not to apply to
Scotland the provisions of the National Parks and Access to the Countryside Act
1949, other than those sections dealing with nature conservation.   To safeguard
the situation in what were felt then to be the most important scenic areas, the
direction required the relevant local planning authorities to submit for scrutiny
by the Secretary of State all applications for developments under the Planning
Acts within the specified areas, and gave the Secretary of State an ability to call
in for determination any which he considered warranted such action.   The areas
affected by these were:

	km^2
Loch Lomond/Trossachs	829
Glen Affric/Glen Cannich/Strathfarrar	673
Ben Nevis/Glen Coe/Blackmount	1579
The Cairngorms	466
Loch Torridon/Loch Maree/Little Loch Broom	1295

The second category of special planning provisions was the designation by planning
authorities in their development plans of Areas of Great Landscape Value where the
authorities themselves chose to operate special development control policies intended
to conserve the particular scenic or landscape interest of the areas so designated.

In addition to the five National Park Direction Areas the Scottish National Park
Survey Committee identified three reserve areas which were:

	km^2
Moidart/Morar/Knoydart	1062
Glen Lyon/Ben Lawers/Schiehallion	362
St. Mary's Loch	466.

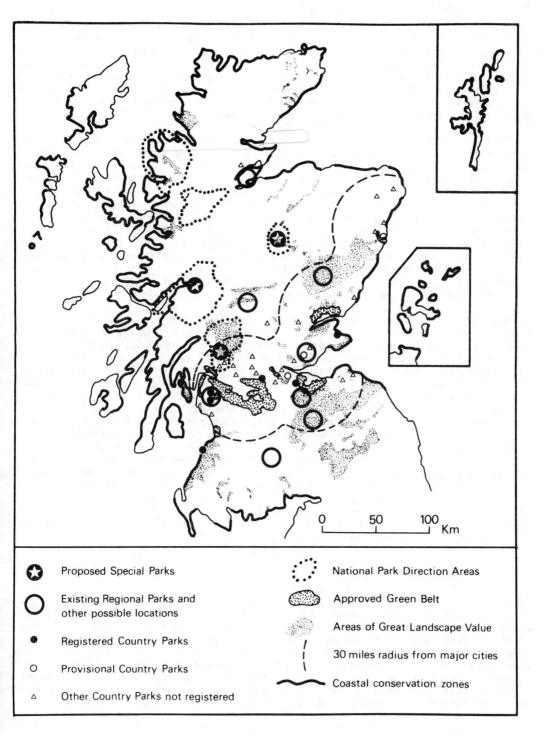

Fig. 8.1 Recreation and Landscape in Scotland

Source: Scottish Development Department

Legend:

- ★ Proposed Special Parks
- ○ Existing Regional Parks and other possible locations
- ● Registered Country Parks
- ○ Provisional Country Parks
- △ Other Country Parks not registered
- National Park Direction Areas
- Approved Green Belt
- Areas of Great Landscape Value
- 30 miles radius from major cities
- Coastal conservation zones

0   50   100 Km

As part of the background survey work for the preparation of the report, A Park
System for Scotland, the Commission prepared a series of descriptive essays on the
five National Park Direction Areas, together with the Outer Hebrides, Knoydart, the
Inner Isles and Galloway. It seemed sensible to begin an examination of the scenic
resources of Scotland with these areas which had commended themselves to earlier
workers in this field and then go on to examine other areas which either suggested
themselves in the course of the survey or were already covered by other conservation
designations signifying a possible scenic interest.

In 1971, in an attempt to further the development of an objective system of scenic
assessment, the Commission published the study A Planning Classification of Scottish
Landscape Resources, prepared by Land Use Consultants. In an annex to that paper
the consultants describe a method for landscape assessment. The Commission tested
this method and came to the conclusion that, although containing a good analytical
approach to landscape, it attempted to combine objective analysis and subjective
judgment in a way which neither produced satisfactory results nor led, as intended,
to evaluative comparisons of different landscape types. The work done by Linton
(1968) in relation to landscape assessment in Scotland and other similar techniques
that have been attempted in Europe and North America were also carefully examined,
but the Commission found none that it felt able to adopt for this review. Accordingly, as already indicated, an approach to the identification of scenic resources
which is based on the subjective judgment of assessors was adopted.

In summary, an attempt has been made to identify scenery which best combines those
features which are most frequently regarded as beautiful. On the whole this means
that richly diverse landscapes which combine prominent landforms, coastline, sea
and freshwater lochs, rivers, woodlands and moorlands with some admixture of cultivated land are generally the most prized. Not all these features occur, however,
in all the areas we have identified. Diversity of ground cover may be absent in
some, but compensated for by especially spectacular landform or seascape. In
Scotland, outstanding examples of such scenery are most frequently found in the
Highlands. It is recognised that many of the more managed landscapes to the south
and east, in areas of intensive agricultural activity, are very beautiful, but it
was found difficult to recognise many of these as being outstanding in a national
or international sense. The Southern Uplands of Scotland were examined most carefully, the subtler landforms and more managed landscapes found there making comparison
with Highland scenery difficult. This is a kind of scenery not replicated elsewhere and one which is very pleasing to the eye attuned to it. Parts of it which,
while not exhibiting the same diversity of form as Highland Scotland, nevertheless
combine pleasing physiography with varied land-use to provide scenery of great charm
and soft beauty, have been identified.

THE APPROACH ADOPTED

In many of the areas identified by the Commission the pattern of settlement is a contributing feature. These areas do not include large towns, but crofting townships,
ancient ecclesiastical settlements and the planned villages of the nineteenth century
improvers often add to the scene. There are exceptions, usually small industrial
towns or villages dependent upon a major industry, but where these occur, they have
been set in the midst of such fine scenery that no useful purpose could be served
by contriving to exclude the settlements from the identified areas. The Commission
considers that this approach, carried out with care and consistency, is a reasonable
course to follow in a subject which has not been found amenable to measurement in
scientific terms.

The method adopted for carrying out the survey was as follows. First, desk appraisals of maps of the Scottish countryside at a scale of 1/50,000 were carried out
to determine the likely extent and character of fine scenery. This work began

with the five National Park Direction Areas then moved on to the other areas already mentioned and subsequently to others which have commended themselves in the course of this survey, or which in the opinion of the surveyors from their extensive knowledge of the Scottish countryside were worthy of study. Although the method suggested by Land Use Consultants was not applied in full, its approach to the analysis of map information was used as the basis for examining topographical maps. Literary sources (see bibliography) were examined for opinions that had been expressed by others about the character of areas being considered. Planning documents produced by local authorities and by national agencies, such as the Nature Conservancy Council and the Forestry Commission, and by private bodies, such as the National Trust for Scotland, were also scrutinised for information on other designations such as Areas of Great Landscape Value, National Nature Reserves, Forest Parks and certain National Trust properties. With this basic appraisal of the likely extent of areas of fine scenery, the surveyors then made field inspections to form opinions as to the extent of landscape tracts which, for reasons of diversity of landform, vegetation and/or ground cover, or other outstanding visual characteristics, appeared to merit recognition as national assets.

THE METHOD ADOPTED

The Commission considers it to be an important aspect of this work that the same surveyors conducted the entire survey, thus providing consistency of view to the whole exercise. Not only did the same team carry out all the field survey work, with never less than two officers undertaking field examination of any particular area, but they reported their findings to a steering group of senior staff which remained unchanged throughout the exercise. The proposals produced in this way were, in turn, subjected to scrutiny by the Commission, which includes members with acknowledged expertise in the fields of assessment of scenic quality and rural land use.

The scenery was deliberately not analysed in terms of its geology, geomorphology, pedology, climate, natural history or cultural history. This is not because these things are unimportant in their influence on the scene, but because enjoyment of fine scenery is based on a perception of the whole which does not depend on more formal kinds of analysis. In particular, a conscious effort was made not to let individual specialisations influence choice: nor was an attempt made to select scenery on a representative basis of all the different types of landscape which occur in Scotland. The Commission hopes that it will be recognised that many attractive areas have had to be omitted in the process of identifying and selecting only that which we consider to be the very best.

Using the procedure and the methods just described, the Commission has identified 40 areas which it considers to be of national scenic significance and which, in the terms used in Chapter 6 of the report A Park System for Scotland, are considered to be of unsurpassed attractiveness which must be conserved as part of our national heritage (Fig. 8.2). Certain of these areas are already under significant recreational pressure and will be proposed as Special Parks when the necessary legislation has been enacted. The bulk, however, are areas which, for the most part, are not under severe recreational or other specific pressures at present. In total, these amount to 12.7 per cent or approximately one-eighth of the land and inland water surface of Scotland. This is not an unreasonably large proportion for a country so renowned for its scenic beauty.

The corollary to selecting only the very best scenic areas for particular care and attention as part of the national heritage is an inference that the remaining areas of countryside are of less importance and there may be disappointment that some places widely acknowledged to be of considerable scenic attractiveness have not been included. However, a great deal of thought has been given to many parts of the countryside which do not appear in the final list and it will, the Commission

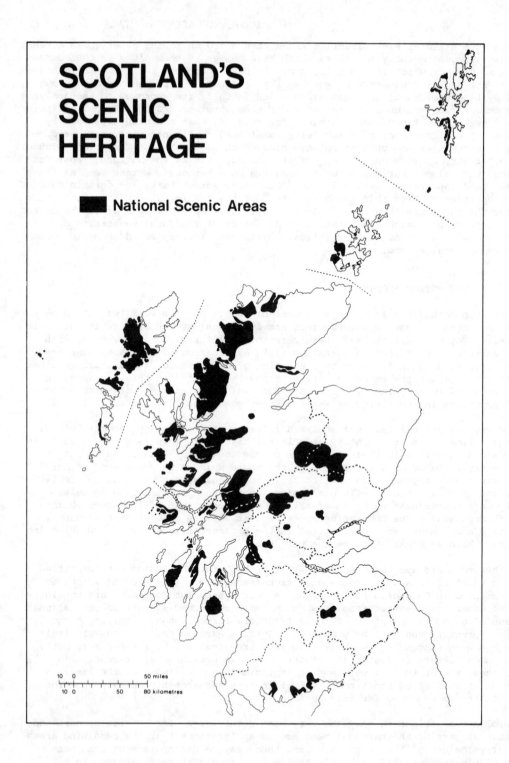

SCOTLAND'S SCENIC HERITAGE

■ National Scenic Areas

Fig. 8.2 National Scenic Areas in Scotland.

hopes, be understood that these areas, while of undoubted scenic merit, do not match
up to the high standards which were set for the areas chosen.   This does not mean
that they are not considered also to be of importance, since many of these areas
will be significant in regional terms.   We believe that they also require conservation strategies and procedures for development control which recognise this significance.   There are also several places which are quite outstanding in themselves,
but which are different in character and scale from the areas in our national list
by virtue of their limited extent and uniformity or their singular nature.   Many
of these are already Conservation Areas in terms of the Town and Country Amenities
Act 1974 or would be suitable for recognition as such.   We hope that policy statements on landscape conservation prepared by Regional Councils will take these
smaller areas into account as well as the wider areas selected as being of national
or of regional significance.

THE WAY AHEAD

So far in this report the Commission's prime concern has been with the selection of
areas of outstanding national scenic significance.   The identification of these
areas is an important first step towards their conservation and appropriate development, but it is no more than a first step.   There must now follow positive action
for their protection and development in ways which take full account of their national
or local significance.   The ways in which this might be achieved are manifold, but
they fall into two broad categories, on the one hand relating to the planning process
and on the other to land management.

In regard to the planning process preliminary discussions have been held with the
Scottish Office and it is expected that the Secretary of State may institute new
planning procedures to safeguard the nation's scenic heritage.   These measures
were foreshadowed in the National Planning Guidelines issued in May 1977 by the
Scottish Development Department and the Commission suggests that they should include, first, an interim policy requiring the notification of certain classes of
planning application within areas of national scenic significance and, second,
longer term proposals for the preparation of appropriate planning strategies and
development control policies.   Various ways exist in the Planning Acts and in the
Countryside (Scotland) Act 1967 for setting up appropriate arrangements for this
purpose and discussions with the Scottish Office and the Convention of Scottish
Local Authorities are in hand.

Responsibility for the preparation of planning strategies and development control
policies is, however, a matter for the Regional and District planning authorities
in the first instance, and it is on these authorities that the main burden of conserving the nation's scenic heritage rests.   Planning authorities are showing
every sign of accepting this responsibility willingly, and with due regard, in
most cases, to the national interest.   The Commission looks forward to assisting
them with advice based upon its broader interest in the whole of the countryside,
extending as it does to over 98 per cent of the land and inland water area of
Scotland.   However, under existing arrangements for planning, the final responsibility for conserving that which is nationally important must lie with the Secretary
of State as the ultimate authority, and it is essential that some procedure is
maintained to ensure that developments in areas of national scenic interest which do
not comply with approved development plans should be referred to him before final
decisions are taken.

The second category of conservation measures relates to land management.   Whilst
the basic appearance of our countryside is determined by its geology and geomorphology
and the effects of climate and light, there is no doubt that the scenic interest is
often greatly influenced by the way in which the land is used, clothing it with a
pattern of vegetation and enclosure to produce that which may be visually satisfying.

Many of the changes which affect the appearance of the countryside are not influenced by the formal planning process, notably changes in agricultural practice itself and changes between agriculture and forestry.   It should be possible to influence such changes of land-use to accommodate the national scenic interest where necessary, while still meeting reasonable requirements for land management, for instance by modifying the shape of new planting to safeguard outlooks from public vantage points or by modifying grazing pressures to increase natural regeneration of woodlands in particular situations.

Where land management is modified to secure the national interest and there is a resultant loss of some financial benefit to the owner or occupier, there is a case for meeting at least part of that cost from Exchequer funds.   Proposals for manage-ment agreements to meet this kind of situation were included in the report *A Park System for Scotland* and management agreements, analogous to nature reserve agree-ments and forestry dedication schemes, should be seen as an important element of the Commission's proposals for the conservation of scenic resources.   Since the Commission made the proposals for management agreements it has had the benefit of substantial public comment and is now of the view that it would not be reasonable to expect the cost of conserving the national scenic interest to be met, even in part, by the ratepayers of local authorities rather than by the nation as a whole through the Exchequer.   It has therefore, proposed to Government that the Commission original ideas should be modified so that management agreements within areas of national scenic interest should be made between land managers and the Commission representing the national interest.   It would still be possible, however, for this machine to be made available to planning authorities in regard to any areas of regional landscape interest which they later seek to identify in their structure and local plans.   Local authority expenditure in this regard should, of course, be eligible for the usual countryside grant at 75 per cent in designated countryside, and to special park authorities at whatever higher rate may be agreed in respect of land falling within Special Parks under the Commission's proposals for a park system.

The Commission now awaits enactment of the necessary legislation and the implemen-tation of the modified planning procedures to enable our proposals to become effective

REFERENCES

Countryside Commission for Scotland (1974). *A Park System for Scotland*.   The Commission, Perth.
Countryside Commission for Scotland (1978). *Scotland's Scenic Heritage*.   The Commission, Perth.
International Union for the Conservation of Nature (1969). *United Nations World List of National Parks and equivalent reserves*.   10th assembly of IUCN, New Delhi, The Union, Morges.
Land Use Consultants (1971). *A Planning Classification of Scottish Landscape Resources*.   Occ.Paper No.1, Countryside Commission for Scotland, Perth.
Leney, Fiona (1975). *Landscape of Scotland*.   Unpublished report for Countryside Commission for Scotland.
Linton, D.L. (1968). Scenery as a national resource in Scotland, *Scott.Geog.Mag.*84.
National Park Committee (1931). *Report* (Addison Report) Cmd.3851, HMSO, London.
National Park Committee (1947). *Report* (Hobhouse Report) Cmd.7121, HMSO, London.
National Park Policies Review Committee (1974). *Report* (Sandford Report), HMSO, London.
Scottish Development Department (1974). *North Sea Oil and Gas; Coastal Planning Guidelines,* The Department, Edinburgh.
Scottish Development Department (1977). *National Planning Guidelines for Large Industrial Sites and Rural Conservation,* The Department, Edinburgh.
Scottish National Parks Survey Committee (1945). *National Parks : a Scottish Survey,* (Ramsay Report), Cmd.6631, HMSO, Edinburgh.

Scottish National Parks Committee and the Scottish Wild Life Conservation Committee (1947). *National Parks and the Conservation of Nature in Scotland*, Report, Cmd. 7235, HMSO, Edinburgh.

Scottish National Parks Committee and the Scottish Wild Life Conservation Committee (1948), *National Reserves in Scotland,* Final Report, Cmd.7814, HMSO, Edinburgh.

CHAPTER 9
ASSESSMENT OF THE PHYSICAL CAPABILITY OF LAND FOR RURAL
RECREATION

M. Johnstone[*] and J. Tivy[**]
*Highlands and Islands Development Board
**University of Glasgow

ABSTRACT

Three aspects of the assessment of physical capability of land for rural recreation
are considered.   Examination of the appropriateness of an anology with agricultural
assessment suggests a continuum from agricultural to scenic assessment, characterised
by decreasing precision of definition of relationships with land properties and difficulties of measuring and testing.   Existing methodologies cover a range of scales
and a variety of resources and use both existing data and field survey;   user-requirements are rarely explicitly defined;   and verbal descriptions, scoring and mathematical equations are used in evaluations, though the validity of the last is doubted.
A systematic methodology is devised for Scottish lochsides, which are divided into
site-types on the basis of slope and vegetation.   Unsuitable sites are eliminated
and the remainder evaluated on the basis of field data.   A comparison of used and
unused sites showed a concentration of the former in the higher capability classes;
exceptions could be explained by extraneous factors of accessibility and demand.

KEYWORDS

Physical capability for rural recreation;   user-satisfaction;   agricultural analogies;
user-requirements;   Scottish lochsides;   site-types.

INTRODUCTION

Rural or resource-oriented, outdoor recreation differs from agricultural land use
and forestry in being a non-productive, non-economic activity in the strict sense
of these terms.   The primary object of the recreationist is the pursuit of mental
and/or physical enjoyment for its own sake.   This involves a wide spectrum of activities, some compatible, others incompatible with other types of land use.   The
good produced - the level or degree of enjoyment attained - is not only difficult to
measure but impossible to cost by direct economic methods.   The factors determining
intensity of recreational use of land and the value of the product, i.e., the recreational experience, are also more complex than in the case of agriculture.   Although the provision of recreational facilities can *make money* and although the rec-
reationists may be prepared to pay a high price for such facilities, no direct correlation can be established between the price paid and the level of enjoyment of the
user.

The post-war increases in leisure time, real income and car ownership, which led to the dramatic growth of levels of recreation and tourism in the 1950s and 1960s are well documented (e.g., Arvill, 1969; Patmore, 1970).   Although the rate of growth has declined following the increase in oil prices in 1973 and the ensuing economic recession, it has been predicted from the evidence available that recreational levels will continue to increase (Dartington Amenity Research Trust, 1976).   The emergence of resource-oriented, outdoor recreation as a significant competitor to the long-established rural land uses of agriculture and forestry has been recognised in the establishment of government-funded bodies charged with the provision of recreational areas and facilities, e.g., the Countryside Commission; in the instigation of national inventories of recreational resources and current use made of them, e.g., Scottish Tourism and Recreation Study (STARS), Tourism and Recreation Information Package (TRIP), Outdoor Recreation Resources Review Commission (ORRRC); and finally in the attempts made by national bodies, local authorities and individual research workers to establish methodologies for the various aspects of recreational land use, classification, planning and management (e.g., Canada Land Inventory, 1969; Dartington Amenity Research Trust, 1976; Goodall and Whittow, 1973); see below.   Studies undertaken to date clearly highlight the need for a *systematic* approach to replace the previously *ad hoc* and often intuitive methods used in recreational planning. This is particularly pertinent to the assessment of the *physical* capability of recreational resources, which is one component of the supply side of the demand - supply equation.   The object of this paper is therefore to examine three aspects of the physical capability of land for recreation:

  i) the extent to which an analogy may be drawn between assessment of capability for recreation and for agriculture;
 ii) methodologies currently available for the assessment of the physical capability of land for recreation; and
iii) exemplification of a methodology designed specifically to evaluate the physical capability of Scottish lochsides for recreational activities, but which could be adapted to a wider range of recreational sites.

SIMILARITY OF LAND CAPABILITY ASSESSMENTS FOR RECREATION AND AGRICULTURE

Many capability methodologies are modelled on the Agricultural Land Classification evolved by the United States Department of Agriculture in 1961, which aimed to classify soils into groups ...*according to their potentialities and limitations for sustained production of the common cultivated crops...* (Klingebiel and Montgomery, 1961, p. 1).   This aim is achieved by grouping soils into capability classes, which represent a range from Class I, in which soils have no major limitation to crop growth, to Class VIII, in which soils have limitations which preclude their use for commercial crop production.   In Great Britain the grouping of soils into capability classes is based on ...*the known relationship between the growth and management of crops and physical factors of soil, site and climate...* (Bibby and Mackney, 1969, p. 1). These relationships are well established for agriculture and the validity of the results of the capability ranking may be tested by measurement of crop yields. In short, agricultural capability is defined in terms of the relationship between land properties and known crop requirements, with the overall aim of maximising crop yield, which is a readily measurable parameter.

On this agricultural analogy, recreational capability is defined in terms of the relationship between land properties and recreational user-requirements, with the overall aim of maximising user-satisfaction.   The requirements of recreational users range from those which are easily isolated and can be given a quantitative value (e.g., depth of water for boating activities) to those which can be isolated but are difficult to define and measure (e.g., shelter), and finally to the much more elusive intangible requirements for pleasing or beautiful scenery.   Definition of these requirements varies both with the individual recreationist and with the level

at which the activity is pursued.   Thus, the range of physical requirements, combined with human perceptions and aspirations, introduces problems in the assessment
of recreational capability which are completely different from those in other types
of land use.

The human element of land assessment for recreation results in a further divergence
from the agricultural *model*.   Whereas the agricultural goal of crop yield is
readily measurable, the recreational goal of user-satisfaction is difficult, if not
impossible to measure, because of the intangibles such as perception, skill, taste
and mood which are involved.

The differences between assessing capability for recreation and that for other types
of land use can best be explained in terms of a continuum, as illustrated in Fig.
9.1.   This starts with assessment of land capability for agriculture where the
relationship between land-use requirements and land properties has been defined and
tested;   passes through forestry, where the relationship is less well understood
because of the longer time-scale during which the crop actually changes the properties
of the land (Selman, 1978);   to recreation where the relationship becomes even less
well defined because of the introduction of human preferences;   and, finally, to
scenic assessment, which is a purely personal judgment of a resource which can change
in character through time and according to the combination of prevailing climatic
conditions, and hence cannot be satisfactorily standardised.   Thus, the introduction
of the human element introduces an inherent problem in any attempt to equate user-
requirements with the properties of the physical landscape.

METHODOLOGIES FOR ASSESSING LAND CAPABILITY FOR RECREATION

Methodologies for assessing land capability recreation have been evolved during the
past thirty years, at scales ranging from national (e.g., CLI, 1969;   Hills, 1966;
Goodall and Whittow, 1973) through regional (e.g., Chubb and Bauman, 1976;   Statham,
1972) to individual case studies (e.g., Floyd, 1974;   Laing, 1974).   The resource
base considered varies from the total land-water complex (Canada Land Inventory
(CLI), 1969;   Statham, 1972) to specific resources such as Forestry Commission
holdings (Goodall and Whittow, 1973), rivers (Chubb and Bauman, 1976), and lakes/
reservoirs (Floyd, 1974;   McLaughlin, 1971;   Laing, 1974;   Johnstone, 1979).
Details of a number of methodologies for assessing capability for recreation are
summarised in Table 9.1.   It is not proposed to discuss here the preliminary stage
of evaluating capability – that of land classification whereby the resource is
divided into land-units which may be considered to be reasonably homogeneous for
recreational activities.   Instead, attention will be focussed on three major aspects
of such evaluation:

a) data inputs;
b) definition of user-requirements;   and
c) methods of evaluating data.

Data inputs to the assessment are inevitably strongly dependent on available sources,
particularly for methodologies, such as the CLI, which are applicable at the national
scale.   Some information, such as certain soil properties and slope of the land,
may be available from existing maps, whereas other data, such as micro-relief, beach
material and vegetation-form must usually be collected in the field.   In general,
methodologies at a national scale, which have been designed as practical planning
tools, tend to rely heavily on available data, whereas studies of smaller areas are
often more academic in nature, with a higher proportion of specifically-collected
field data.   The CLI is filling the gap in information on recreational resources
by mapping relevant site-factors at two scales (1:250,000 and 1:50,000).   In Scotland inventories of the location of recreational *activities* and of the capacity of
associated facilities are underway, e.g., the TRIP data bank and STARS, but there is

Method of evaluation of data	Definition of Capability Classes	Subclasses	Assumptions
Descriptive interpn. based on 'known relationships between the growth & management of crops and physical factors of soil, site and climate'.	Class 1 few limitations suitable for a range of crop types; class 8 unsuitable for any crops.	Specify type of limit- ations.	Moderately high level of management; ignores access and location.
Descriptive; capability classes based on combinations of limit- ing factors present; analysis at local and regional scales.	Class A no limitations for a particular group of activities; Class F unsuitable.	"	Based on inherent resource properties; assumes the user has completed a field training programme.
Descriptive; classes defined according to their ability to engender and sustain recreation.	Class 1 suitable for a range of activities; has high use-tolerance.	Specify positive features present.	Sound level of management; land modifications not considered; uniform demand & accessibility; assessment independent of present land use.
"	"	"	Sound recreation manage- ment; uniform access to the lochshore.
Quantification of constraints to capability in the form of an equation.	Capability Class defined by score.	–	–
Scoring system applied to slight, moderate and severely limiting factors.	"	–	–
Scoring system applied to limiting factors; computed by 'RIVERS' programme.	Score expressed as % of the maximum possible score.	–	–
Quantification of limiting factors, including accessibility in the form of an equation.	Score converted to a value on a 1 – 100 scale	–	Restricted to supply side only.
Scoring system applied to weighted limiting factors.	Class 1 highly suitable; Class n unsuitable.	–	Present land use does not affect rating.
"	"	–	Sites of high capability require min. management.
"	"	–	Uniform accessibility.

TABLE 9.1 Comparative Summary of Selected Capability Methodologies

Author(s) *	Aim of study (or relevant part of study)	Resource base	Area of study	Type of land unit	Data inputs	Data sources
Klingebiel* Montgomery, 1961/Bibby & Mackney, 1969	'to group arable soils according to their potentialities and limitations for sustained production of the common cultivated crops' (Bibby and Mackney, p1).	Arable soils	US/GB	Soil group/ soil series	Attributes of the resource base	Soil maps
Hills, 1966a Cressman, 1968	'to evaluate the relative capability of landscapes to attract and sustain intensive recreational use' (Cressman p1).	All land types	Canada	Physiographic units; min.16 mi^2	"	Field & map data
Canada Land Inventory, 1969	'to provide an inventory of natural outdoor recreation resources based on the quantity of recreation which may generated and sustained/unit area of land under perfect market conditions' p7.	All land types	Canada	Physiographic; 1:250,000	"	"
McLaughlin 1971	To determine the capability of the resource base to support and sustain recreation.	Loch and lochside	Loch Earn Scotland	Physiographic; 1: 10,560	"	"
Statham, 1972	To evaluate recreation capability as an input to deciding between alternative land uses.	"	North Yorkshire Moors	Based on car park capacities	Car park capacities	"
Floyd, 1974	To develop a systematic approach for the selection of optimum recreation sites near to reservoirs.	Shore of reservoir	Lake Loco (Texas)	Soil groups	Attribs. of the res. base	"
Chubb and Bauman, 1976	'to develop a river evaluation technique which would be useable in a wide variety of situations' p3.	Rivers & river shores	Michigan	Mile river lengths	"	Air photos fieldwork, agencies
Goodall & Whittow, 1973	To define a practical method of assessing the potential of FC holdings for various recreational activities.	FC holdings	Selected forests in GB	Transects from random sample areas	" & questionnaires	Fieldwork & sports bodies
Laing, 1974	To evaluate the recreational capability of the Loch Carron area.	Lochside	Loch Carron	Physiographic 1: 10,560	Attribs. of res. & interviews	Fieldwork
Potter, 1976	To evaluate the recreational capability of Loch Rusky and Lake of Menteith	Lochsides	Two lochs	"	"	"
Morgan 1977	To evaluate the recreational capability of Loch Ken, using the method evolved by the author	Lochside	Loch Ken, river Dee	"	Attribs. of the resource	"

* See Bibliography for sources of information.

Source: Johnstone, 1979.

LAND USE	Agriculture	Forestry	Recreation	Scenic Assessment
	-------------------------------------→			
DEFINITION OF USE(R) - REQUIREMENTS	Most precise			least precise
	-------------------------------------→			
DEFINITION OF RELATIONSHIP BETWEEN USE(R) - REQUIREMENTS AND LAND PROPERTIES	Most precise			least precise
	-------------------------------------→			
TESTING THE VALIDITY OF CAPABILITY RANKINGS	Possible			impossible
	-------------------------------------→			

Fig. 9.1 Model of Land Capability Assessment for Different
Land Uses

no comprehensive inventory of recreational *resources* available for use by local authorities and other planning organisations.

In considering the level of detail of such inputs, Steinitz and others (1969), in a valuable review of sixteen methods of resource analysis, point out that *a resource evaluation which combines a variety of data from a variety of sources is only accurate to the level of its coarsest component. Consistency in scale between purpose and data and indeed among the various data themselves is inadequately treated in most if not all of the methods which we have studied.* (Steinitz and others, 295).

Thus, it is important that the level of detail of the various data inputs are systematised in relation to the aim of the method. Ideally, inventories should consist solely of objective measurements, but in practice the data inventory is usually a mixture of *objective measurements and subjective evaluation.* While the inclusion of subjective assessments is inevitable and does not invalidate the method, it is important that such assessments should at least be systematically applied, with an adequate explanation of the method used so that it can be reproduced by users other than the designer.

Definitions of user-requirements form the basis of the capability evaluation, with optimum user-requirements defining sites with high capability, and minimum user-requirements defining sites with low capability, as shown in Fig. 9.2. The concept of the *limiting factor*, defined as *a key element which exerts such a negative influence on the potential for developing a particular kind of recreation area or enterprise that it poses problems that are difficult or impossible to overcome* (United States Department of Agriculture, quoted in Tivy, 1972, 11-12), is commonly adopted to identify the degree of limitation imposed by important user-requirements. It would seem to be equally valid to include an assessment of *enhancing factors*, defined as key elements which exert such a positive influence on the potential for developing a particular kind of recreation area or enterprise, that they may be considered to be advantageous to the area. Ideally, both optimum and minimum user-requirements should be determined for each activity in order to define the physical conditions of the highest and lowest capability classes. In practice, user-requirements for land-based activities are, as already indicated, difficult to define in any form,

Consider one type of recreational activity taking place on one site-type.

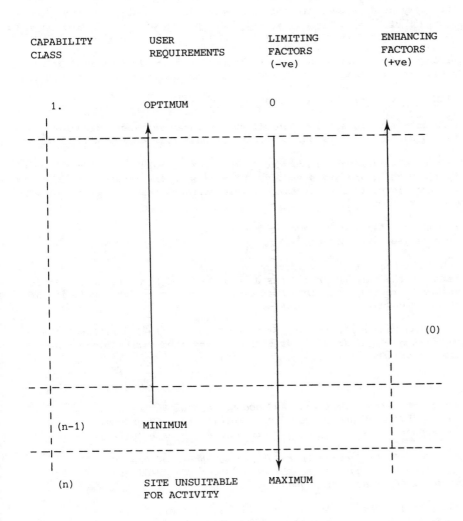

Source: Johnstone, 1979.

Fig. 9.2 Idealised Model of Capability Ranking Systems

and it has been found impossible in most cases to distinguish between optimum and minimum requirements (Johnstone, 1979). As a result, user-requirements are rarely explicitly defined in methodologies for assessing capability, with the notable ex- ceptions of Goodall and Whittow (1973) and McLaughlin (1971). This basic component of land capability assessment for recreation clearly warrants further attention.

Evaluation of Data.   All such methodologies do, however, contain an *implicit* definition of user-requirements in the method adopted for evaluating the data.   Three
methods are currently used to evaluate data on recreational capability to define capability classes.   The first comprises verbal descriptions of such classes, as used
in the CLI and in Hill's system and illustrated in Table 9.2.   In these cases implicit definition of user-requirements is least precise and it is difficult to all-
ocate a capability class to sites which do not accord to any of the verbal descriptions.   Secondly, in an attempt to be more precise and systematic, scoring systems

TABLE 9.2 Model or *Benchmark* Class E Site for Camping and Bathing

Class E Lands Having a Moderately Low Capability for Intensive Recreational Activi-
ties Engendered by Bathing Beaches and Adjoining Grounds for Camping and Services

Class E lands in this series have a moderately low average capability for the com-
bination of family bathing and group camping activities.   Under natural conditions
these lands are restricted to low intensity of use for a number of reasons, of which
the following are examples:

i) One of the features has a very severe limitation.
ii) A total of three medium limitations.

Thus, in spite of the moderately low average capability, it is possible that either
the bathing beach or the camping ground has a relatively high capability.   It is
therefore possible to increase the intensity of use, even to a high level, if suf-
ficient effort is expended.

The following are the common benchmarks for Class E lands in which either beach or
camping grounds with no significant limitations are combined with the other having
very severe limitations.

Map Symbol

Bh	*Wet beach over 66 feet wide and occupying over 8 chains*
EG	*per 20 chains of shoreline is covered with rock fragments.*
d	*The supporting service grounds are of Class A or B quality.*
B	*Over 90% of the grounds lying within 40 chains of the*
EGt	*shoreline have short slopes between 15 and 30% gradients.*
d	*Beach is of Class A or B quality.*
B	*The grounds lying within 40 chains of the shoreline are*
EGw	*covered with peat or muck 1 to 3 feet deep. The beaches*
d	*are of Class A or B quality.*
B	*Area of quality camping and service sites restricted in*
EG	*size to 5 to 10 acres per 20 chains within 20 chains of*
d	*the shoreline.*

Source: Hills, 1966, 16-17.

---

have been adopted in some methodologies (Table 9.3).   Each site factor is allocated
a score reflecting the degree of limitation or enhancement it imposes, and the capability class is defined in terms of the sum of scores, which are also weighted to
reflect the relative importance of different site factors.   This method has the
advantage that user-requirements are, if only implicitly, more precisely-defined,
and that an infinite range of possible combinations of scores is covered.   Thirdly,

TABLE 9.3 Capability Evaluation for Camping and Caravanning

Data Category	Score +1	0	-1	-2	-3	-4	-5	Multiplier
3 Aspect		S/SW/SE	W/E		NW/NE		N	3
4 Flood hazard		Never		Occasional		Frequent		4
5 Shelter	Very sheltered						Very exposed	1
7 Max. gradient		0-10°	11-15°	16-20°	21-25°	26-30°	>30°	1
7 Inhib. vegn.		Short grass/woodland	Tall grass		Low shrub	Arable	Wetland/shrub	1
15 Width of site-type		>30m	26-30m	21-25m	16-20m	10-15m	<10m	3
16 Gradient		0-4°	5-6°	7-8°	9-10°	11-12°	>12°	4
17 Macro-relief		Planar	Gently undulating		Undulating		Strongly und/Narrow terraced	1
18 Micro-relief		ΔH = 0-5cm	6-10cm	11-15cm	16-20cm	21-25cm	>25cm	3
19 Veg. form		Short grass	Woodland/Tall grass		Low shrub		Arable/shrub/wetland	3
19 Treespacing (av)		>10m	8-10m	5-8m	4-6m	2-4m	0-1m	1
20 % Rock/stones		0-10%	11-15%	16-20%	21-25%	26-30%	>30%	2
21 Depth org. layer		1-4cm		5-6cm		7-8cm	>8cm <1cm	1
22 Soil texture		L/SCL/SL	CL/SCL/SiCL/LS/S (not loose)		SC/SiC/Loose S		O/C *	2
23 Soil drainage		Excessive/free		Imperfect		Poor	Very poor	4
24 Soil depth		>25cm	21-25cm	16-20cm	11-15cm	6-10cm	<5cm	2
25 % stones		0-10%	11-20%	21-30%	31-40%	41-50%	>50%	½
26 Size stones		Very small		Small	Medium		Large	½

* L = loam   Si = silt   C = clay   S = sand   O = organic material

two methodologies, those of Statham (1972) and Goodall and Whittow (1973), have gone one stage further in defining capability classes in terms of a mathematical equation, as exemplified in Table 9.4.   In this way not only the relative importance of site factors, but also their interaction are taken into consideration.   Each site factor is assigned a score which is fed into the equation and the final score is used to determine the capability class of that site.

TABLE 9.4 Definition of Recreational Potential Index, P_R
for Forestry Commission Holdings

$$P_R = P_1 + P_2 + P_3$$

where:

$$P_1 = 1/4 \ (T + (K\%T) + W - (R + E))$$

P_1 = Topographic score
T = Terrain score
K%T = Undulation score
W = Water score
R + E = Amplitude of relief score

$$P_2 = B + H + 4S - O$$

P_2 = Mantle factor
B = Broadleaf score
H = Tree height score
S = Spacing of mantle score
O = Open land score

$$P_3 = \frac{(C + Ap + D) - Aw}{xy}$$

P_3 = Climate/Access/Uniqueness factor
C = Climate score
Ap = Local inaccessibility score
D = Dispersion score
Aw = Inaccessibility of water from roads score
xy = Uniqueness score

Source: Goodall & Whittow, 1973.

Conceptually, this last method is the most advanced since it presents the most re-fined model of site factors contributing to user-satisfaction. In practice, however, the difficulties of defining user-requirements makes such precise manipulation of data of questionable validity. There is, therefore, a need to choose a method of evaluating data which is consistent with the level of accuracy with which data can be defined and collected.

A METHODOLOGY FOR ASSESSING THE PHYSICAL CAPABILITY OF LOCHSIDES
FOR RECREATIONAL ACTIVITIES

The following method of assessing the physical capability of Scottish lochside sites for recreational activities was developed in the course of a study undertaken between 1974 and 1977 by the Department of Geography, University of Glasgow for the Country-Side Commission for Scotland, on the recreational use of lochsides in Scotland (Tivy, in press). It has been designed with the needs of on-site planners and managers in mind and, in contrast to the normally intuitive process of capability assessment for recreation, the methodology is *systematic* in nature, although (as previously mentioned) it does contain subjective elements. It has general applicability to fresh-water lochsides throughout Scotland and it is envisaged that it may be used:

a) in assessing the capability of a particular site for a specific activity;
b) in determining the most suitable site for a particular activity;
c) in assessing the activities for which a lochside is most suited when developing a previously unused loch and its perimeter for recreation; and
d) in assessing activities for which a lochside is most suited when there is heavy and conflicting use.

The lochside was defined as *that area of land extending from the water's edge to either:*

   i) a road, track or railway within 100 m; or
  ii) a major change in vegetation or landform; or
iii) for a distance of 100 m if (i) or (ii) does not apply.

One hundred metres was chosen as the maximum width of lochside on the basis that most rural recreation is car-based, and the average recreationist does not walk more than this distance from his car.   Since the lochside is such a narrow zone parallel-ing the lochshore it is clear that the method is applicable to the more detailed end of the scale in comparison to that of CLI which operates at the national scale. The first stage of the procedure is to divide the lochside, which can vary from wet-land to a vertical rock face, into units or site-types which are reasonably homogene-ous in terms of the dominant slope and dominant form of vegetation - two attributes which were identified as being consistently the most important in influencing user-requirements.   In addition, shore features, defined below, are used to refine the classification further.   The classification of site-types, which is summarised in Fig. 9.3 is open-ended, and allows further features to be incorporated as necessary.

Shore Features

   i) *Beach* (B) The zone of accumulated inorganic material (mud to boulders), extending from summer (or lowest sustained) water-level to the highest point reached by storm waves.

  ii) *Rocky shore* (R) A shoreline of rock *in situ*, less than 10 m wide.

 iii) *Wetland Fringe* (W) A shoreline fringe of wetland vegetation 1-3 m wide.

  iv) *Cliff* (C) An extremely steep land-face formed of sand, clay, boulder clay or peat, located at the back of the shore.   The height varies between 0.25 and 3 m, the face may be planar or undercut and is usually without vegetation.

   v) *Strip* (S) A narrow (less than 5 m wide) facet of gentle slope located between the water's edge, wetland fringe, rocky shore, beach, or cliff and a bank, or the primary facet which has a steeper gradient.

  vi) *Bank* (K) A land-face of moderate or steeper gradient behind the water's edge, wetland fringe, rocky shore, beach or cliff; of limited width (less than 10 m); usually vegetated; and succeeded on the landward side by a site-type of less steep gradient.

 vii) *Embankment* (E) A man-made slope, of moderate or steeper gradient; varying in height from 1 - 10 m; composed of unconsolidated material or stone; and usually associated with a road, railway or reservoir.

After the site-types have been designated a preliminary sorting is undertaken where-by those site-types where slope and vegetation-form are totally unsuitable for a particular activity are eliminated from further assessment, using Fig. 9.4, which is based on a set of user-requirements determined for each activity.

For those sites which have not been eliminated detailed field data are recorded along three transects perpendicular to the lochshore, as shown in Fig. 9.5.   These data are evaluated using capability matrices, as exemplified in Table 9.3 for camping and caravanning.   Like Fig. 9.5, this table is based on a set of recreational user-requirements derived from a number of sources.   The method of scoring employed is considered to represent the best compromise between somewhat vague verbal des-criptions and the questionable precision of expressing capability in terms of a

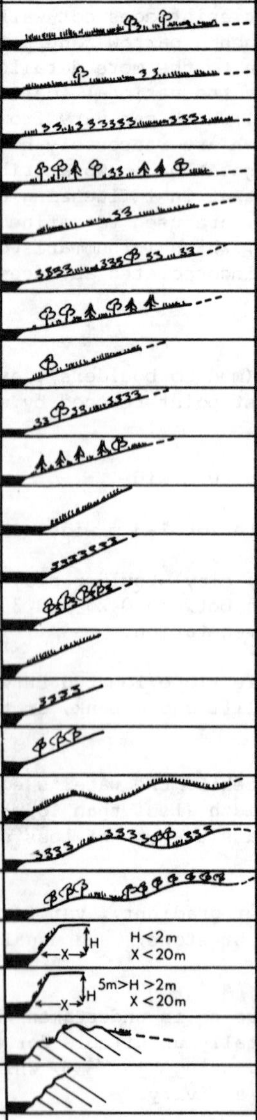

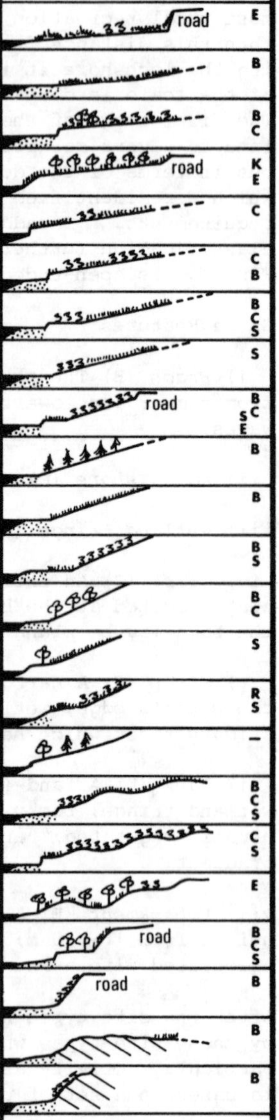

	BASIC PROFILE	Essential Features		POSSIBLE SHORE FEATURES							EXAMPLE OF PROFILE with Shore Features
		Dom. Slope	Dom. Veg. Form	Beach (B)	Rocky Shore (R)	Wetland Fringe (W)	Cliff (C)	Strip (S)	Bank (K)	Embank -ment (E)	
1		G	M		✓	✓	✓			✓	road E
2a		G	F	✓	✓	✓	✓		✓	✓	B
b		G	S	✓	✓	✓	✓		✓	✓	B C
c		G	T	✓	✓	✓	✓		✓	✓	road K E
3a		M	F	✓	✓	✓	✓	✓	✓	✓	C
b		M	S	✓	✓	✓	✓	✓	✓	✓	C B
c		M	T	✓	✓	✓	✓	✓	✓	✓	B C S
4a		S	F	✓	✓	✓	✓	✓		✓	S
b		S	S	✓	✓	✓	✓	✓		✓	road B C S E
c		S	T	✓	✓	✓	✓	✓		✓	B
5a		VS	F	✓	✓	✓	✓	✓		✓	B
b		VS	S	✓	✓	✓	✓	✓		✓	B S
c		VS	T	✓	✓	✓	✓	✓		✓	B C
6a		ES	F	✓	✓	✓	✓	✓		✓	S
b		ES	S	✓	✓	✓	✓	✓		✓	R S
c		ES	T	✓	✓	✓	✓	✓		✓	–
7a		M	F	✓	✓	✓	✓	✓	✓	✓	B C S
b		M	S	✓	✓	✓	✓	✓	✓	✓	C S
c		M	T	✓	✓	✓	✓	✓	✓	✓	E
8	H<2m X<20m	>M	F S T	✓	✓		✓	✓			road B C S
9	5m>H >2m X <20m	>M	F S T	✓	✓		✓	✓			road B
10		G–S		✓	✓		✓	✓		✓	B
11		S–VS		✓	✓						B

Slope : **G** = Gentle (0-5°), **M** = Moderate (6-10°), **S** = Steep (11-15°), **VS** = Very Steep (16-20°), **ES** = Extremely Steep (OVER 21°)

Vegetation Form : **M** = Wetland, **F** = Grass and Forbs, **S** = Shrub and Dense Woodland, **T** = Open Woodland

Fig. 9.3 Classification of lochside site-types (Source: Johnstone, 1979).

USE of SHORE COMPONENT / ACTIVITY	OFFSHORE GRADIENT FOR ACCESS INTO WATER BODY	SHORE FOR ACCESS	SHORE FOR PURSUIT OF ACTIVITY	BACKSHORE FOR ACCESS	BACKSHORE FOR PURSUIT OF ACTIVITY
CAMPING • CARAVANNING • CAR–BASED PICNIC ON BACKSHORE minimum area 9m²/pitch					A 2a 2c 3a 3c B 4a 4c 7a 7c C 1 2b 3b 4b 5a 5b 5c 6a 6b 6c 7b 8 9 10 11
WALKING • } BACK PONY TREKKING } SHORE NATURE TRAIL NATURE STUDY • minimum length ½ mile					A 2a 2c 3a 3c 4a 4c 7a 7c B 5a 5c 6a 6c C 1 2b 3b 4b 5b 6b 8 9 10 11
ORIENTEERING					A 2b 2c 3b 3c 4b 4c 5b 5c 6b 6c 7b 7c B 7a C 2a 3a 4a 5a 6a 8 9 10 11
WALKING • } SHORE PONY TREKKING • minimum length ½ mile			A B Sa Sc B K C WF R C Sb	A 2a 2c 3a 3c 4a 4c 5a 5c B 6a 6c 7a 7c C 1 2b 3b 4b 5b 6b	
PICNICKING SHORE			A Sa Sc R B K C B C WF Sb	A B .. C	
BANK FISHING	moderate or steeper off–shore gradient		A WF C K R B Sa Sb Sc B C	A B .. C	
SWIMMING SUB–AQUA (without boat)	shallow, non–shelving off–shore gradient	A R B B CK Sa Sc C WF Sb		A B .. C	
BOAT LAUNCHING	shallow or moderate off–shore gradient which shelves	A B B K C Sa Sc C WF R Sb		A B .. C	

KEY : A   Lochside component is HIGHLY SUITABLE, in its present state, for the activity.
      B   "   MODERATELY   "   "   "
      C   "   UNSUITABLE   "   "

For key to site-type codes see Fig. 9.3.

Fig. 9.4 General Assessment of the Capability of Lochside
Components for Recreational Activities

mathematical equation. This methodology inevitably involves subjective assessments but, since these are carried out within a systematic framework, the degree of reproducibility of the method is increased. In addition, each stage of the methodology is self-contained so that, if the method of data evaluation were to be modified, it would not be necessary to alter the stage of data collection as well.

Testing the Results of the Capability Rankings

In contrast to the methodologies mentioned earlier, an attempt was made to assess the

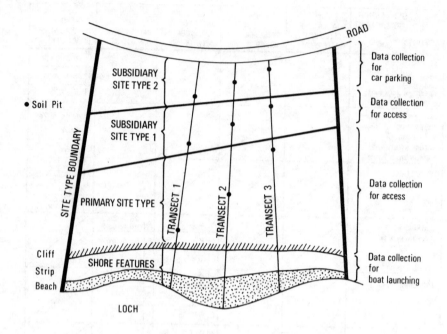

Source: Johnstone, 1979.

Fig. 9.5 Method of Field Data Collection

validity of the rankings of particular sites.   The rankings of sites known to be used for particular activities were analysed, *on the assumption that actual use is a reflection of capability*.   This method was used as a compromise to the conceptually-desirable, but practically difficult ideal of measuring user-satisfaction. Table 9.5, in which the capability rankings for samples of both used and unused lochside sites are compared, suggests that used sites tend to be weighted towards the top end of the capability scale, whereas unused sites cover a wider range of capability classes.   However, certain sites which, according to the methodology, should be totally unsuitable for the activity received high capability rankings. Such anomalies can be explained in terms of factors such as accessibility and demand which are extraneous to that of physical capability, thus demonstrating that this is only a small part of the land assessment procedure.

CONCLUSION

It is thus obvious that the basic differences between recreational and other types of rural land use pose particular problems for land assessment for the former purpose.   The physical attributes of the site are only one set of factors determining its recreational capability.   The lochside case study, presented here, does not purport to provide a complete answer to the methodological problems involved in assessing physical capability.   Rather it illustrates the difficulties involved in attempting to satisfy some of the criticisms of alternative methods by designing a flexible and *systematic* methodology appropriate to the level of data available and to the scale of analysis involved.

TABLE 9.5 Number of Cases of Each Capability Class for Used and Unused Recreational Sites

Capability Class / Activity	1 S(U)	2 S(U)	3 S(U)	4 S(U)	5 S(U)	Class Range S	Class Range U
Backshore							
Camping & caravanning		3 (5)	4(8)			2-3	2-3
Car-based activities	1 (2)	2(12)	1			1-3	1-2
Picnicking	4	8 (6)	5 (5)	(2)		1-3	2-4
Walking	(4)	(22)	1 (8)			3	1-3
Pony trekking	(1)	(11)	(22)	(1)		-	1-4
Orienteering		(2)	(11)	(7)	(1)	-	2-5
Nature study	1 (2)	(15)	(16)	(1)		1	1-4
Access to shore	(3)	10 (5)	6(10)	3	1	1-4	1-3
Shore							
Picnicking	9(18)	4(18)	2 (6)	(1)	(2)	1-3	1-5
Walking	2 (6)	2(34)	(1)	(5)	(1)	1-2	1-5
Pony trekking	(8)	(33)	(3)	(6)	(1)	-	1-5
Bank fishing	(1)	1(22)	2(23)	(2)		1-2	1-4
Boat launching	(1)	4(17)	5(13)	1 (9)	(1)	2-4	1-5
Swimming	1 (2)	9(23)	(13)	(3)		1-2	1-4

Key: S - site used for recreational activity
(U) - site unused for recreational activity

REFERENCES

Arvill, R., (1969). *Man and Environment*, Penguin, Middlesex.
Bibby, J.S. and D. Mackney, (1969). *Land Use Capability Classification*, Soil Survey of Scotland, Technical Monograph No. 1, Aberdeen.
Canada Land Inventory, (1969). *Land Capability Classification for Outdoor Recreation*, Report No. 6, Ottawa.
Chubb, M. and E.G. Bauman, (1976). *Assessing the Recreational Potential of Rivers*, Paper at 72nd Ann. Meeting of Assoc. Amer. Geogr, Mimeo, New York.
Cressman, E.M., (1968). *Methodology for Ontario Land Inventory*, Ontario Department of Lands and Forests, Toronto.
Dartington Amenity Research Trust, (1976). *Planning for Sport, Outdoor Recreation and Tourism : Strategic Issues*, Vol.1, Countryside Commission for Scotland and others, Battleby.
Floyd, W.E., (1974). *Selection and Evaluation of Land Resources for Outdoor Recreation Areas Adjacent to a proposed Reservoir*, M.Sc. Thesis, Stephen Austin State University, Texas.
Goodall, B. and J.B. Whittow, (1973). *The Recreational Potential of Forestry Commission Holdings*, Report to the Forestry Commission, University of Reading.
Hills, G.A. (1966). *Definition of Capability Classes and Bench Mark Sites for Recreational Land Inventory*, Research Branch, Ontario Department of Lands and Forests, Maple, Ontario (Mimeo).
Johnstone, M., (1979). *A Methodology for Assessment of the Physical Capability of Scottish Freshwater Lochsides for Recreation*, Ph.D. Thesis, University of Glasgow.
Klingebiel, A.A. and P.H. Montgomery, (1961). *Land Capability Classification*, U.S. Department of Agriculture and Soil Conservation Service, Agric. Handbook 210, Washington, D.C.
Laing, A.I., (1974). *An Evaluation of the Capability of the Loch Carron Area for Shore-based Recreational Activities*, Undergraduate Dissertation, University of Glasgow.

McLaughlin, B.P., (1971). *Recreation : A Planning Methodology with Special Referenc* to Loch Earn, M.Sc. Thesis, Heriot-Watt University, Edinburgh.

Morgan, S.M., (1977). *The Recreational Capability of Loch Ken and the River Dee,* Undergraduate Dissertation, Middlesex Polytechnic, Enfield.

Outdoor Recreation Resources Review Commission, (1962). *Outdoor Recreation for Amer* Government Printer, Washington, D.C.

Patmore, J.A., (1970). *Land and Leisure,* David and Charles, Newton Abbot.

Potter, S., 1976). *The Capability of Lochshores for Recreation,* Undergraduate Dissertation, Middlesex Polytechnic, Enfield.

Selman, P., (1978). *The Application of Soil Survey and Land Capability Classificati* Monograph 1, Glasgow School of Art.

Statham, D., (1972). Capability analysis for recreation in the North York Moors. *Recreation News Supplement,* August, 23-27.

Steinitz, C., T. Murray, D. Sinton and D. Way, (1969). *A Comparative Study of Resou. Analysis Methods,* Graduate School of Design, Harvard University.

Tivy, J., (1972). *The Concept and Determination of Carrying Capacity of Recreationa. Land in the USA,* Countryside Commission for Scotland, Occasional Paper No. 3, Per*

Tivy, J., In Press. *The Effects of Recreation on Freshwater Lochs Throughout Scotla* Countryside Commission for Scotland, Battleby.

Tourism and Recreation Research Unit, (1975-1977). *Scottish Tourism and Recreation Study Reports,* Report Nos. 14, 18, 19, 20, 25, 26, 27, Department of Geography, University of Edinburgh.

U.S.D.A., (1966). *Guide to Making Appraisal of Potential Outdoor Recreation Develop* ments, Washington D.C. (Quoted in Tivy, J., 1972).

DISCUSSION

Comment by G. Dickinson, University of Glasgow.

The subject matters of the papers by McCarthy, Turner and Johnstone are linked by their location at that end of the continuum of land resource assessment which Johnstone and Tivy describe as being characterised by inherently decreased precision in definition and measurement.   They differ in the scale of assessed areas, their functional roles and in relationships between evaluation and management procedures. Further examination reveals certain problems in land assessment for conservation and recreation worth fuller discussion.

The problems, and even their basic definition, are variable.   This is in part related to the scale of the study areas, but is much more due to the nature of conservation and recreational land use, users requirements, interaction with other land users and management policies.   If the assessment of physical capability of land for rural recreation avoids some of the difficulties associated with user preferences, the study by Johnstone and Tivy indicates the needs for precision, comparabilit between sites and as high a degree of objectivity as is possible, presenting a considerable research challenge.   Whilst the assumption that actual use is a reflectio of capability is debateable at a national scale, the results of the testing of the ranking scheme indicate the value of this approach.   Somewhat similar difficulties are encountered in assessment of land for nature conservation.   As McCarthy states, the principal problems lie not so much in the collection of data (though it is fair to point out that there remains here considerable conceptual, methodological and logistical problems), as in the evaluation of data.   Furthermore, assessment may have to be expanded to include human factors influencing the conservation value of an area; these latter factors include accessibility and consequent user pressures, compatibility with existing land uses and viability of management procedures.   They are remarkably similar to some of the factors influencing recreational values.   The presumption of clear policy on objectives for nature conservation by the administering agency is thus critical, because of this interaction between physical resource characteristics and human evaluations of these.   The balance between conservation based on ecological principles and conservation based on management practice must profoundly influence development of appropriate methods of land assessment.

The role of value judgment inevitably becomes even more significant in any attempt to assess scenic heritage; indeed, both terms have strong perceptual inferences. However, as Turner points out, the task of the Countryside Commission for Scotland is essentially practical.   The initial approach developed by Land Use Consultants (1971) used in the Commission's 1978 review has been criticised by Turner (1975, 151) on the grounds that the constraints imposed on tract comparison and the varia- bility apparent in surveyors' assessments very seriously limit its value.   To what extent this adversely influences the overall findings of the review is debateable, though inclusion of field-based comparative evaluation does allay some objections. The final statement, though based on a hybrid scheme, does seem to provide a workable basis for initial planning purposes.   Landscape planning,as Turner has pointed out, faces difficulties because of the inherent problems of subjective judgment in land- scape evaluation (Turner, 1975, 160).   Nevertheless it is evident that the pressing needs for national recreational land-use planning require sensible, broadly-based land assessment for this purpose.

Some important general issues are raised by these papers.   Factor weighting (often subjectively based) as a means of influencing the inputs to assessment schemes re- mains a contentious issue, though field-based testing of ranked sites is a valuable check on such systems.   The debate on consumer attitudes in assessment is likely to continue.   The inclusion of perceptual preferences in evaluation methods, as has been advocated by Penning-Rowsell (1974) presents great difficulties, and it may be that public participation can best be included at the planning rather than the eval- uation stage.   The need for landscape assessment, such as is indicated by the Countryside Commission for Scotland in its 1974 report *A Park System for Scotland* (paragraph 6.2, 26-7) is such as to commend the use of appropriate land assessment methods in conservation and recreation planning, and fully offset the arguments against any such appraisal.   Pressures on land in Scotland will increase and con- tinued work towards national rural planning based on sound evaluation must continue. The three general proposals of Appleton (1975, 123) remain proper objectives for the development of evaluation techniques.   These were improvement of empirical techniques, critical evaluation of results and continued development of theoretical bases.   These three papers indicate the considerable progress being made in these directions.

REFERENCES

Appleton, J., (1975). Landscape evaluation : the theoretical vacuum, *Trans. Brit. Geogr.*, 66, 120-3.
Countryside Commission for Scotland, (1974). *A Park System for Scotland*, Battleby, Redgorton, Perth.
Countryside Commission for Scotland, (1978). *Scotland's Scenic Heritage,* Battleby, Redgorton, Perth.
Land Use Consultants, (1971). *A Planning Classification of Scottish Landscape Resources*, Countryside Commission for Scotland, Occ. Pap. 1.
Penning-Rowsell, E.C., (1974). Landscape evaluation for development plans, *J. R. Tn. Plann. Inst.*, 60 (10), 930-4.
Turner, J.R., (1975). Applications of landscape evaluation : a planner's view, *Trans. Inst. Br. Geogr.*, 66, 156-61.

Reply by Dr. Johnstone.

I disagree with the implication in Dr. Dickinson's comment that *assessment of phy- sical capability of land for rural recreation avoids some of the difficulties assoc- iated with user preferences.*   We indicated in the section of our paper on

Definitions of User Requirements that these are difficult to define, and that this component of land capability assessment warrants further research.

CHAPTER 10

PLANNING AND LAND ASSESSMENT IN SCOTLAND - ROLE OF THE RURAL
LAND USE INFORMATION SYSTEMS WORKING PARTY

G.A. Lyall
Scottish Development Department

ABSTRACT

The Rural Land Use Information Systems Working Party is considering services of
information on rural land use, methods of handling data and initiatives by individual agencies.   It has produced a map catalogue, data inventory and user-requirements survey, and a consultant's report has found that greater co-operation in data
collection was desirable and that a rigorous pilot project was needed to test the
benefits, costs and use of an integrated system.   A project has been mounted in the
Dunfermline and Kirkcaldy District to identify the operational difficulties for day-
to-day work and decision-making and to investigate alternative methods of data handling in the context of user-requirements.   The project is due for completion in
July 1980.

KEYWORDS

Statutory planning; data for rural planning problems; co-ordination of data collection; Rural Land Use Information System Working Party; pilot project; costs and
benefits; alternative methods of data handling.

INTRODUCTION

As a basis for planning procedures there is a need to have an overall picture of land
use in Scotland and of the changes that are taking place.   This requires an assessment of areas of countryside subject to pressure for development and change, including areas sensitive to pressure and areas which can absorb pressure.   Planning procedures in Scotland have evolved over time in response to physical, economic and
social problems.   The end result is the current planning system which includes three
levels of government (national, regional and district) and the preparation of five
kinds of plans (national guidelines, regional reports, structure plans, local plans
and financial plans).   These all feature in the rural planning system and represent
both a demand for, and a production of, information.

At the national level the Scottish Development Department has published a series of
National Planning Guidelines on development and conservation issues of national importance.   These provide an indication of national policies on urban and rural planning, and in particular on the siting of large industrial plant and include appraisals

107

of the suitability of land for agriculture and for forestry, as well as indications
of areas that are important for scenic and wildlife conservation.

The regional authorities are responsible for broad strategic planning for their areas
and have each prepared a Regional Report which represents a corporate survey and
policy statement on all major needs and expenditure programmes for which the regional
authority is responsible.   Currently, the regions are at various stages of preparing
Structure Plans for their areas.   The structure plan represents a comprehensive
appraisal of the physical planning issues and a coordinated set of policies for urban renewal, industrial expansion, communications, rural development and resource
conservation.

Local plans are prepared mainly by District Authorities and are the basis of decisions on proposals for site development and land-use changes, and they provide an
interpretation of the broader national and regional strategic plans to the local
scale.   They are prepared after a detailed survey of the trends and needs of the
area and after consultations with local residents and interest groups.

THE RURAL PLANNING PROBLEM

There is a wide variety of frequently inter-related issues affecting land assessment
and rural planning: agriculture, forestry, tourism and recreation, winning of mine-
rals and aggregates, land for large industrial sites, roads and conservation of wildlife and scenic areas.   There is therefore a need for an integrated approach to survey work, policy formulation and programme implementation.   This is particularly
important since not only does each of the levels and types of planning mentioned
earlier require a wide range of information from a wide range of sources, but there
is also an output of information from each stage in the planning process which other
stages can use.

There is therefore a dynamic inward and outward flow of information from the planning
process.   The data sources for the assessment of these issues are also widely scattered in a variety of forms throughout central and local government and the rural
land-use agencies.   Consequently, there is a pressing need to coordinate the data
held by the various agencies so that they can be more efficiently used and better
land assessment and rural planning achieved.   Some examples of these issues and
inter-relationships will serve to illustrate this point.

Rural planning and urban planning share common ground in the urban fringe, the sub-
urban semi-urban area around the edges of towns and cities throughout Scotland.
Parts of this urban fringe are formally designated as Green Belts in an attempt to
reduce the damaging effects of urban expansion on the adjacent countryside.   To
identify these effects and monitor the results of planning policies requires cooperation between farming interests, landowners, developers, conservation groups,
housing, transport and recreation authorities.   Urban development problems are
found far beyond the urban fringe in some city-regions, crossing several administrative boundaries, census areas and other statistical divisions.

Demand for scattered dwellings, tourist facilities and some industrial developments
are found in the countryside.   In analysing and predicting these pressures on rural
land, planners need wide-ranging data on, for example, the demand for second homes,
trends in tourism, rural employment structure, and the site requirements of industry.
In order to assess the effects on a rural area corresponding data are needed on communications, soil quality, landscape characteristics, recreational resources, climate,
water supplies and drainage patterns.

Significant changes are also evident in agricultural methods and productivity, the
nature and extent of upland farming, and the design of farm buildings.   At the same

time there is an extensive programme of afforestation underway, increasing competition for plantable land, and prospects for the growth of wood-processing industries over the long-term.   These are inter-related trends, and they generate a need for compatible data, efficient arrangements for the exchange of such data and coordinated research.   They also require information on the suitability of land for agriculture and for forestry.

There are also social issues of particular concern for rural planning.   The reduction of jobs in the primary sectors, the ageing of the population structure in the remoter areas, the falling numbers of pupils in rural schools and the economic problems of rural bus services all have repercussions on planning policies, local financial resources and the balance between conservation and the promotion of development.

RURAL LAND USE INFORMATION SYSTEMS WORKING PARTY

This need for coordination of widely-held and varied information has been recognised, particularly with the development of the new planning processes, and as the various agencies supplying data have been reorganising and improving their data collection to take account of computer technology.   Consequently in March 1976 the Rural Land Use Information Systems (RLUIS) Working Party was established with a remit to: examine the comprehensive information needs of the member agencies and to consider the longer-term feasibility of computer-based systems, as a means of achieving better organisation and exchange of information.   The terms of reference developed from this general remit are to:

  i. consider the chief information sources on rural land use and their availability;
 ii. examine the method of collection, storage and dissemination;
iii. determine any information gaps;   and
 iv. examine recent initiatives by individual agencies on computerised data systems, and the scope for securing a better flow of information, and consider the long-term possibility of a compatible information system for use by Government and local authorities.

The member agencies of the Working Party are: the Department of Agriculture and Fisheries for Scotland, the Countryside Commission for Scotland, the Forestry Commission, the Institute of Geological Sciences, the Macaulay Institute of Soil Research, the Nature Conservancy Council and the Scottish Development Department.   The Department of the Environment, the Scottish Tourist Board and Fife Region have been added subsequently.

Appendix 1 lists the member agencies of the Working Party and some of the current uses they make of computer systems.   The existence of the Working Party has already made the agencies aware of each others' interests in this field and consequently lessened the likelihood of different systems being developed in a widely-divergent manner.

Since the Working Party was established it has produced a series of reports and papers to fulfil the terms of reference.   The most important of these are:

1. Survey of Universities, Colleges and Local Authorities: all colleges, universities and local authorities were circulated to inform them of the existence of the Working Party and to find out any similar research that was being done.

2. Map Catalogue: A list of all maps held by the member agencies was compiled as an aid to the exchange of information.   It contained information on the source of the maps, their scales and whether they were published, could be reproduced or were confidential.

3. Data Inventory: An inventory of all data held by each agency, listing the form in which the data are held (mapped or statistics), the method of handling and storage (manual or automated), information on scale and area covered, and the original source of the data.   (Most of the reports are for the use of the Working Party only but the Data Inventory has been sent to the respondents in the survey in (1) above).

4. User Requirements Survey: A survey of the requirements of member agencies for information; systems for storing and manipulating data (whether computers were used or not); and identifying gaps in information coverage.

5. Fife Map Window: A small-scale exercise in digitising maps to inform members of the working party of some of the problems, benefits and uses of computer mapping.

6. Consultant's Report: C. Chulvick of the Planning Data Management Service (PDMS) was engaged as consultant to the Working Party soon after it began work and was asked to prepare a report explaining the methods of data handling used by the agencies and their benefits and shortcomings, and to examine the feasibility of moving towards an automated and integrated information system for rural land use data.   This report included some assessment of the computer software and hardware that might be necessary, where a system might be located and how it might be operated.   From the wealth of information contained in this report two main conclusions can be highlighted: the present piecemeal approach by member agencies to data collection, storage and handling is unsatisfactory, and greater overall cooperation is essential; and a further more rigorous pilot project is necessary to test the costs, benefits and uses of a fully-integrated information system for data on, or related to, rural land use.

PILOT PROJECT

Having accepted the recommendation from the Consultant's report, the Working Party proceeded to establish a pilot project.   There were three main elements to be decided:

1. the area to be studied;
2. the aims of the project - the range and scope of the work and the end product; and
3. the structure of the project.

1. In choosing the area there were basically two options, an urban fringe area or a remote rural area.   It was decided that an urban fringe area would demonstrate the widest range of planning policy issues and include most of the data required by member agencies for planning in the remoter areas.   Consequently, Fife Region and in particular the Districts of Dunfermline and Kirkcaldy were chosen as the study area.

2. It was agreed that the aims of the project should be to focus on the kinds of problems and issues with which individual agencies have to deal on a day-to-day basis and for policy and decision-making.   Furthermore, the project should investigate the alternative methods available of handling data and their relative costs (for manual and computer systems) related to a clear specification of user-requirements. Finally, it should enable conclusions to be drawn about which data sets require what degree of resolution, level of accuracy and detail, and the costs, benefits and uses of establishing an integrated information system.   As a by-product, the project should enable agencies to appraise better the problems and costs of restructuring and regularly-updating their data holdings for incorporation in an information system, whether manual or computerised, centralised or decentralised.

3. It was particularly important to decide the structure of the project since an

integrated system could become totally unwieldy, incorporating too many data sets.
The first step was to agree a list of data enclosed (Appendix 2), comprising 60 items
and covering basic topographic data, information on land-use and statistical data
sets; data on land capability are thus a minor (though important part) of possible
data sets.   It was agreed that the first part of the project should be data collection and this should be divided into three parts to enable comparisons of cost to be
made.   Existing manual methods of collecting data should be costed and assessed.
It was also proposed that mapped data should be recorded by aggregation to grid squares
using techniques available in PDMS and by digital mapping.   Other data would be lo-
cationally referenced.   The digital mapping element is particularly important since
Ordnance Survey is investigating the use of digital cartography, and digital maps
offer the most flexible use of data in that mapped information can be readily associated with statistical data in the computer and previously-difficult analyses become
possible.

The second part of the project is the analysis of the data collected.   This will take
the form of a series of specific problems related to the issues outlined earlier.
Apart from providing answers to specific planning issues in the test area, the analysis stage will demonstrate what can be done with an integrated computer information
system which cannot be adequately done with the present diverse nature of information
storage.   Another important product of this part of the project will be the preparation of special software to handle the routines required, as costs permit, and identifying what other software is required, which cost and time do not permit in the
pilot project.

The final part of the project will be the preparation of reports highlighting the
problems encountered.   To these will be added an assessment of the costs and benefits of an integrated information system, the uses to be made of it and the form that
such a system might take.   This end product will provide the arguments to demonstrate
the feasibility or otherwise of creating an integrated information system and some
points are advanced here to promote discussion.

Data Collection

Some of the primary data, on topography, geology and soils,are of interest to all
agencies whereas some are more specialised and of limited interest and may not be
suitable for inclusion in a centralised information system.   Data such as the agricultural returns may present problems of confidentiality which it may be difficult
to safeguard in a centralised system.   The costs of recording some data by digital
means may be too high for the use required of them whereas some data such as the
topographic and primary land use data may have little value if generalised to grid
squares.   Finally, the amount of data to be collected will be the subject of discussion.   Some of the data sets may be excluded and others could no doubt be added,
but the use to be made of each data set and the costs of providing it and keeping
it up-to-date will have to be adequately justified before it is included in a centralised system.

The Structure of a System

The pilot project will identify the computer software and hardware necessary to
create an operational information system.   The location of such a system will lead
to discussion.   Should it be centralised, with all agencies supplying data to a
central data bank, or should each agency develop its own data bank?   There are
likely to be economies in a central data bank but problems of confidentiality, up-
dating, accuracy and accessing the data argue against it.   The great benefit of a
centralised system is the opportunity to extract a wide range of general and special
data, and to analyse many unexplored relationships which might reveal unexpected
features of the past trends, present characteristics and future prospects of an
area.   It would be particularly useful in comparing different assessments of land
for different purposes.

Establishing a centralised data bank would be expensive both in time to create the computerised data sets and in the cost of so doing. It may be, therefore, that the easy option, at least initially, will be for each agency to develop its own computerised information system as time and cost permit, but in a form compatible with other agencies so that current and potential relationships between the dispersed data sets could be identified and explored.

A problem of a cooperative effort in creating an information system is consideration of the future. It is difficult to foresee what use the information collected now may be put to in five or ten years time. Will the same data sets be required and will the analyses required be the same? There is no doubt that much will be unchanged but the changes may be significant enough to require expansion or contraction of the data base. Whatever system is created, flexibility of operation will be essential.

This pilot project is an important step forward in the collection and handling of data on rural land use for rural planning and rural land assessment. Whatever the eventual outcome, the cooperation evident in the Working Party between Central, Regional and District Government and the Rural Land Use Agencies demonstrates the will to improve the collection, storage and use of rural land-use data.

APPENDIX 1

The following lists briefly the member agencies, their current use and intended use of computer techniques in data handling. It also lists other interested parties involvement in computer data handling.

Member Agencies

Scottish Development Department - The Central Research Unit undertakes analytical work using census data. Use is made of LINMAP (Department of the Environment), GIMMS and CAMAP to produce maps of census material from 1 km² data based on the centroid of each enumeration district. The Scottish Office Computer Service (SOCS) is also used to carry out cluster, principal component and regression analyses.

Countryside Commission for Scotland - CCS is one of the sponsors of PDMS/TRIP which is a computer-based data handling system for information on tourism and recreation It handles point and line data and data by 1 km² grid and can produce lists, tables and maps. It has now been operating as a service for 3½ years with a management team to run that service (e.g., request for data, input of new data).

Department of Agriculture and Fisheries for Scotland - Agricultural census returns are stored on computer tape and statistical analyses are carried out by SOCS.

Forestry Commission - Data on FC forests are held on magnetic tape. The 1965 Census of Private Woodlands consists of a 15 per cent sample by 1 km² and is recorded by centroid; this data is also held on magnetic tape. Private Dedicated and Approved woodlands records are being put in machine-readable form, a task which is to be complete in 1980/81. FC hopes to undertake a survey of other private woodlands and store the data in a computer system for presentation in tabular form for aggregated areas, e.g., counties or districts, which will correlate with information already held. FC has also been involved with TRIP/PDMS.

Nature Conservancy Council - NCC makes use of the Institute of Terrestrial Ecology's computer and that at the Biological Records Centre, Huntingdon, for recording and manipulating some of the data it collects. It has also analysed some data using TRIP/PDMS.

Institute of Geological Sciences - IGS has its own digitiser and flat bed plotter and its main unit of collection is point data (borehole and geochemical data). It is currently involved with the Experimental Cartography Unit in digitising geochemical data and experimenting with digitising geology maps. It is continuing to investigate methods of making even greater use of the automated facilities available to it.

Macaulay Institute for Soil Research - MISR is experimenting with capturing soil data by recording on voice tape then digitising and punching the information. The CAMAP system has been used to map the information by a 1 km² grid.

Ordnance Survey - OS is currently digitising maps at 1:1250 and 1:2500 scale and is producing derived maps at 1:10,000 and 1:25,000 scale. It is also investigating the feasibility and demand for digital maps at the 1:50,000 scale.

Department of the Environment - There are several initiatives on computer techniques in DOE. The Local Government Directorate is particularly involved in research on the restructuring of the OS digital data base for use in management information systems so that it may be efficiently used by others for analytical work as well as producing maps.

There have also been a number of commissioned research projects, mainly investigating the uses of computer maps and data and the operations of information systems so far developed, e.g., automated digitising of information, mapping and computers in DOE, local authority information systems, classification of developed areas and users' perceptions of maps.

DOE operates its own computer mapping service called LINMAP and uses it mainly for analysis and presentation of data from the population censuses.

Fife Region - The Region has a computer system collecting all planning application statistics and has created a variety of other computer files including population census, employment and unemployment data and valuation rolls.

Scottish Tourist Board - STB is one of the main sponsors of PDMS (see CCS).

Outside Body

Natural Environment Research Council - NERC is running three inter-related projects using the digitising capabilities of the Experimental Cartography Unit. It is intended to produce an ECO-Base for Great Britain, digitising the topographic base and adding natural environment data. ECU is currently digitising the IGS for the Regional Geochemical Survey, from north of Scotland southwards and for the Institute of Hydrology, the River Network Data, and has completed an ecological survey in Shetland for ITE.

APPENDIX 2 : RURAL LAND USE INFORMATION SYSTEMS PILOT PROJECT

INITIAL LIST OF DATA AND SOURCES

Ref. No.	Data Items	Type of Data	Scale of Data	Source Departments
1	Topographic contours	lines	1:50,000	Ordnance Survey
2	Coastline (high tidal level)	"	"	" "
3	Rivers and lakes	"	"	" "
4	Postal code areas	boundaries	:	Post Office

Ref. No.	Data Items	Type of Data	Scale of Data	Source Departments
5	Regions and districts	boundaries	1:50,000	Ordnance Survey
6	Borehole data	points	1:10,000	Institute of Geological Sciences
7	Solid geology	boundaries	1:50,000	" " "
8	Drift geology	"	"	" " "
9	Soil types	"	"	Institute of Soil Resear●
10	Soil condition	"	"	" " " "
11	Land use capability	"	"	" " " "
12	Farm-land quality	"	"	Department of Agricultur●
13	Landform class	grid	"	University of Edinburgh
14	Beach type	"	"	"
15	Natural habitat	"	"	Nature Conservancy
16	Marginal agricultural areas	boundaries	"	Department of Agricultur●
17	Farm units	"	1:10,000	" " "
18	Forestry capability	"	1:50,000	" " "
19	Agricultural land use	"	"	" " "
20	Existing woodland	"	"	Forestry Commission
21	Land taken for forestry	"	"	" "
22	Forest recreation areas	"	"	" "
23	Sand and rock deposits	"	"	Institute of Geological Sciences
24	Old mining areas	"	1:10,000	" " "
25	Subsidence areas	"	"	" " "
26	Derelict land	"	"	Scottish Development Department
27	Built-up areas	"	1:50,000	" "
28	Designated countryside	"	"	" "
29	Major industrial sites	points	"	" "
30	Defence land	boundaries	"	Ministry of Defence
31	Electricity lines and pipe-lines	lines	"	Electricity Boards
32	Water and sewerage schemes	"	"	Regional Authorities
33	Transport networks	"	"	Scottish Development Department
34	Development plan zonings	boundaries	"	District Authorities
35	Land taken for building	"	1:10,000	" "
36	Designated green belts	"	"	" "
37	Nature reserves	"	"	Nature Conservancy Counc●
38	Sites of scientific interest	"	"	" " "
39	National Trust Land	"	"	National Trust
40	Country Parks	"	"	Countryside Commission
41	National scenic areas	"	"	" "
42	National planning guidelines	"	1:500,000	Scottish Development Department
43	Historic buildings	points	1:25,000	" "
44	Recreation facilities	"	"	Countryside Commission
45	Population census	statistics	"	Registrar General
46	Employment structure	"	"	Department of Employment
47	Development applications	points	"	District Authorities
48	Development notifications	"	"	" "
49	Planning appeals	"	"	" "
50	Countryside grants	"	♥	Countryside Commission
51	Land for development	boundaries	1:10,000	District Authorities
52	Agricultural census	statistics	"	Department of Agricultur●
53	Forestry census	"	"	Forestry Commission
54	Traffic volumes	"	1:50,000	Scottish Development Department

Ref. No.	Data Items	Type of Data	Scale of Data	Source Departments
55	Water supplies	statistics	1:50,000	Scottish Development Department
56	Climatic records	"	"	Meteorological Office
57	Statistical units	boundaries	"	Regional Authorities
58	Pedestrian routes	lines	"	Countryside Commission
59	Private estates	boundaries	"	" "
60	Land sales	statistics	"	Scottish Development Department

DISCUSSION

Comment by R.M. Boyle, University of Strathclyde.

Planners are sometimes labelled as parasites living off the life-blood of other people's toil, often interfering in the natural progress of change.   In terms of planning for rural areas perhaps another metaphor is more appropriate: impoverished scavengers eeking out a meagre existence on the scraps of information scattered infrequently around by a host of healthy animals, many listed by George Lyall in Appendix 1 of his informative paper.

As the paper began with a review of the role of planners in the field of land assessment, it is salutory to mention two points to put the humble role of the planner into perspective.   Firstly, while planning is concerned with making plans, one can argue that the real powers lie in the control of development.   But what are the powers to control development of rural, especially agricultural land?

Quoting from the Town and Country Planning (Scotland) Act, 1972, Section 19 (1) states:

development means the carrying out of building, engineering, mining or other operations in, on, over or under land, or the making of any other material change in the use of any buildings or other land

However, Section 19 (2) goes on:

the following operations or uses of land "shall not" be taken for the purposes of this Act to involve development,
including:
the use of any land for the purposes of agriculture or forestry and the use for any of those purposes of any building occupied together with land so used.

Secondly, just how important is rural land in terms of statutory plans?   A quick glance at the final version of the Strathclyde Structure Plan, recently published, would lead an outsider to believe that Argyll, Lanarkshire and Ayrshire didn't exist! Admittedly, there are 5 short paragraphs on Remote Rural Areas - but no mention of agriculture or land.   Similarly, in the Chapter entitled *Environment* there is no reference to rural land, *per se*.   And finally, the important section on Resources only deals with land in terms of areas of derelict land.

Is land, especially in rural areas, an important component of planning?   I remain unconvinced.

Turning to the substance of the paper, George Lyall has correctly pinpointed one of the major problems, namely the dispersed and disparate nature of the data available. Taking a wild guess, the problems encountered in rural data are possibly twice as complex and confusing as in urban situations.   One can only applaud the efforts of RLUIS to clear a path through the dense undergrowth of those disparate data holdings.

Nevertheless, I think a word of warning is required.   What appears to be an up-to-data listing of data holdings may, in reality turn out to be an amalgam of half-truths out-of-date surveys and unreferenced data.   This was found when a similar study was done for the ACTISP project (Application of Computer Techniques to Information Systems for Planning).

I was encouraged by the serious consideration that had been given to the question of automated handling of data.   Again drawing upon the experience from ACTISP could I make a plea that whatever system is used in the pilot and subsequently recommended, the people involved in the pilot record and document the problems, often administrative and procedural, which are likely to arise from the design of a useful data bank on rural land use.

Concerning the points raised for discussion, my following remarks may stimulate further debate.   In the design of any information systems there are always what are termed *nuts and bolts* and *bells and whistles*.   This is certainly the case in the design of both housing and development control information systems.   Is there not therefore a case for using the pilot to determine as far as possible:

(a) *Core Items* (the nuts and bolts):   essential data which are central to the operation of the system.   It might be difficult to choose the core elements, but cost might not be the only parameter.   When chosen, this core material would require constant up-date, cleaning and enhancement.   The core might then be developed by the addition of,

(b) *Peripheral Items* (the bells and whistles):   data added where available or where additional costs can be justified in terms of specialist use.

But whatever structure is adopted, the system must be flexible enough to cope with change.   Data of interest today is too often redundant tomorrow;   what is ignored today may be absolutely crucial tomorrow.

Turning to Lyall's last point, the structure of the system, it might be worthwhile bearing 3 points in mind.

1. Dispersed information systems may lead to duplication of software which are costly, problematic and inefficient.

2. To adopt a dispersed structure may create more administrative and procedural barriers, the very problem RLUIS had to overcome.

3. Evidence from other applications of EDP suggests a move towards a *centralised main-frame* handling basic data and software, with a range of *mini's* linking into the main-frame, yet capable of adding the bells and whistles, be it data or analysis, particular to the agency or user concerned.

This half-way house might also fit into my suggested structure for the data base to handle the wide variety of data needed to fuel a useful information system for rural land use.   I only hope that RLUIS gets the support it requires and that planners and others are able to tap into all the data required to make meaningful decisions about rural land use.

Reply by G.A. Lyall.

It is increasingly considered negative for planners' activities, especially in rural planning, to be thought of as primarily concerned with development control.   Positive policies are as yet largely voluntary, and optional to the need seen by the authority concerned, but management agreements with landowners or developers may be all the more effective for that.   The Countryside Commission's report *A Study of Management Agreements* makes useful comparison of the relative strengths and weaknesses of the range of alternative means available for securing a public interest in land.   Statutory planning controls are only one of them.

Secondly, rural land is becoming an increasingly important component of many of the current round of Structure Plans!   Strathclyde is not surprisingly an untypical example, where the priorities and the approach are primarily urban.   The Lothian Structure Plan, which is the most advanced towards approval in Scotland, demonstrates quite a different approach to policy making.

CHAPTER 11
DYNAMIC MODELLING OF LAND-USE ASSESSMENT

J.N.R. Jeffers
Institute of Terrestrial Ecology

ABSTRACT

Land-use assessment is not completed by the production of maps showing the assignment of areas to various categories, for these can do little to integrate conflicting assessments; assessment is only the beginning of a complex process of developing policies for realising the full potential of land. Optimising allocations
within constraints can be achieved by mathematical modelling techniques, which also
facilitate discussion of objectives and solutions. Experience with such techniques
suggests that agencies are often not fully aware of such conflicts, that many constraints can be relaxed, that the widest range of solutions should be generated,
that the search for acceptable strategies should begin as soon as possible, and that
the approach facilitates identification of needed research and improved data collection.

KEYWORDS

Dynamic modelling; optimisation; land-use assessment; conflicting; land-use
policies; range of feasible solutions; land-use allocations.

This symposium on land assessment in Scotland has been concerned with the concept of
land capability and the development of a working system for the improvement of the
use and conservation of the natural resources of Scotland. From information about
the soils, vegetation, present land use, and climate of identified regions of Scotland, we expect to be able to find a better way of planning the use and conservation
of natural resources and of assessing the potential of land for a variety of possible uses. These uses include agriculture, forestry, water, wildlife conservation,
recreation and visual amenity, which, in our Western system, are the responsibilities
of separate agencies. Nevertheless, we have tended to assume that the assessment
of land capability in Scotland provides (or will provide) a neutral basis from which
rational judgments may be made about the relative balance of the various uses that
will be encouraged, or permitted, in a given area. Unless our concept of land
capability is capable of meeting such a requirement, we have no standards for comparison of alternative land-use strategies.

We have also tended to assume that the outcome of a land capability assessment is
necessarily a map or some other spatially-oriented display, enabling any agency or

land owner to determine the capability or potential of any given parcel of land. Such maps have already played a prominent role in the Canada Land Inventory (1970), for example.   Certainly, some visual representation of land capability assessment in Scotland will be essential.   Most people, whether scientists or layment, have highly-developed visual imagery, and will only be happy when the basic concepts of our land capability are displayed in a visual form.   The latest advances in conventional cartography, in computer-based cartography, in video displays, in microfilm and microfiche, will all be utilised to represent our classification and assessment of land capability.

However, our capability and land-use assessment is not completed by the production of maps showing the assignment of areas of land to the various categories, even where these maps are held on computer files, or in some other medium, to facilitate access and consultation.   We still need an ability to examine the consequences of the policies that are adopted by those agencies having an impact upon land use.   More particularly, and more urgently, we need ways of revealing the conflicts between the policies of separate agencies against the background assessment of land capability.   No one classification is likely to reveal the complexity of these conflicts, and we need, therefore, the ability to show the wide variety of options which is available for an integrated land-use policy.   A very large number of maps would be necessary to represent the full range of options available for future land use.

This approach assumes, of course, that the basic factors of land use capability are to be kept separate from the assessment of the strategies of land use which are to be adopted in the light of political, social, and economic constraints.   Such an assumption, however, is not to be taken for granted, as many proposed schemes for land-use survey and assessment, in the United Kingdom, in Europe and elsewhere, have been compromised by a subjective choice of sample units, a scheme of classification based on a *priori* judgments, and methods of data collection and evaluation which do not permit a valid analysis and re-evaluation of the assessment if any of the external constraints are altered.

A simple example may be useful at this point in the argument.   It is often assumed, in discussions of rural land use, that third-class agricultural land is first-class forestry land.   The assumption arises because, historically, agriculture has been given priority to the extent that forestry, and certainly afforestation, has been relegated to land which is only marginally suitable for agriculture.   In an ecological sense, the assumption is wrong - land which has the highest capability for agriculture also has the highest capability for forestry (and probably also for wildlife conservation and recreation).   We should not automatically assume, therefore, that land with the highest capability for agriculture will always be used for agriculture.   Future shortages of energy may lead to a changed evaluation of the relative needs for forestry and agriculture on areas of high biological productivity. We cannot, therefore, allow the pre-judgment of relative values to constrain our representation of land capability.

Although the first priority in the development of a coherent policy for land use is the creation of an awareness of the conflicts between the policies of the many separate agencies which have an impact on rural land use, the next stage must inevitably be the resolution of those conflicts.   In the past, the resolution of conflicts in land use has most frequently been achieved by a forced dominance of the policies of one or more agencies, supported by fiscal (especially taxation) measures.   The worst effects of closed-option resolution of this kind have perhaps been moderated by the inertia (and, sometimes, plain good sense) of private individuals who still own a very large proportion of Great Britain.   Secure in the knowledge that change will come if they wait long enough, private landowners have often been content to sit tight and resist policies with which they disagree!

The policy for land use which has emerged from undeclared conflicts has three principal properties. First, it is based on a faith that present trends will continue into an indefinite future and that the response of ecological, economic and social systems will be related to the amount of investment in a simple and direct way. Second, it envisages an economic and political commitment to recover the costs of investment, even if there is no irreversible loss of resources which cannot be renewed. Third, it is assumed that any failure which is due to lack of understanding of fundamental relationships can be rectified, at least temporarily, by further investment. If any of these assumptions is subsequently found to be wrong, the usual reaction to a wrong choice of dominant policy is to use additional investment, or additional resources, to correct the original mistakes. The alternative course of reversing the original decision and accepting the loss of investment is politically and psychologically unacceptable to policy-makers.

Walters (1975) has characterised this process as a specific hypothesis: *There exists a special kind of pathological decision behaviour that can arise in perhaps all sequential decision problems. This behaviour has its roots in a very human characteristic: we do not like to admit and pay for our past mistakes. The main charcteristics of the pathological behaviour are increasing investment, increasing costs for system maintenance, foreclosure of decision options, and decreased ability of the managed resource system to absorb qualitatively-similar natural perturbations.*

The remedy for this trap, set by the need for sequential decisions, is the frank declaration of conflict between the policies desired by separate agencies. It then becomes possible to explore the consequences of adopting one or another policy, or some compromise between many of the policies, against a background of factual information about the climate, physiography, soils, vegetation, land use and ecology of the area for which a coherent policy is required. The exploration of consequences merges imperceptibly into the generation of a wider range of options where there is sufficient flexibility in the ways in which information on land capability, and on the various facets contributing to the assessments of capability, can be utilised to test the probable effects of decisions and the feasibility of alternative options. In general, such flexibility can only be obtained by the methods of dynamic modelling which have recently been developed for land-use planning. These methods have been described by Swartzman and Van Dyne (1972) and British research in this field has been summarised by Batty (1972). The use of mathematical models for the solution of any kind of problem is not, of course, without its critics (see, for example, Gifford (1971) and Hoos (1972)), especially where one suspects the critic knows rather little mathematics. Nevertheless, systems analysis, as the orderly and logical organisation of data and information into models, followed by the rigorous testing and exploration of the models necessary for their validation and improvement (Jeffers, 1976), has begun to have a major impact on research and practice of land-use and regional planning. The word *model* in this context is defined as a quantitative representation which, if complex, may require algebraic and symbolic manipulation.

Elsewhere (Jeffers, 1979), a distinction has been made between the kinds of models we need for research purposes and those which are more suitable for regional and land-use planning. In research, our intellectual and academic preference is for complex models, dependent upon relatively advanced mathematical forms for their assumptions, formulation and solution. While attractive to the mathematician and to mathematically-orientated natural scientists because of their power and flexibility, such models are frequently almost uninterpretable to the general public, committees of elected representatives and decision-makers, and *opaque* even to scientifically-trained administrators and advisors of land-use agencies. While we may use such models in research, we certainly cannot use them as a means of communication to even an informed general public. There is, however, an alternative class of models for which the basic mathematical concepts are easy to explain and comprehend. These models do not attempt to represent physical, chemical and ecological processes, but, instead, concentrate on the problem of finding an optimum combination of a (perhaps large) series of entities when constraints are placed on the maximum or minimum numbers of some or all of those entities. Confusingly, this class of models falls within the general heading of mathematical programming, probably because, although the formulation and basis of such models is easy to understand, the search for an optimum solution under various constraints involves some difficult and, until the advent of computers, tedious calculation. Indeed, the solution to such problems was one of the best kept secrets of the Second World War.

In mathematical terms, the general form of this class of model is as follows:

Maximize   :   F $(x_1, x_2, x_3, \ldots x_n)$

by setting $x_1, x_2, x_3, \ldots x_n$

subject to : $g_1 (x_1, x_2, x_3, \ldots x_n) = 0$

$\quad\quad\quad g_2 (x_1, x_2, x_3, \ldots x_n) = 0$

$$\begin{array}{ccc} \cdot & \cdot & \cdot \\ \cdot & \cdot & \cdot \\ \cdot & \cdot & \cdot \end{array}$$

$\quad\quad\quad g_m (x_1, x_2, x_3, \ldots x_n) = 0$

In our application, the $x_1, x_2, x_3, \ldots x_n$ will frequently be areas, and the function F $(x_1, x_2, x_3, \ldots x_n)$ will represent the multiplication of those areas by various coefficients so as to derive a total *yield* in terms of biomass, value, or investment.   The constraints $g_1 ( )$, $g_2 ( )$, etc., represent limitations which are placed upon the possible combinations of $x_1, x_2, x_3, \ldots x_n$.

The difficulty of obtaining a solution to the purely mathematical problem of finding an optimum (i.e., maximum or minimum) value of the objective function within the constraints depends on the form of the objective and the constraint functions.   The simplest solutions occur where these functions are linear, but solutions can also be found, with more or less difficulty, for non-linear functions, where the x-values vary discontinuously, and where the x-values are qualitative rather than quantitative.   An introduction to these optimisation models is given by Converse (1970), and the general application of linear programming models is well described by Greenberg (1978).   An application of the methodology of linear programming to regional strategy-making has been described by P.M. Kenjins (1974), and an example of the simple transformation of the linear programming model to allow for the explicit recognition of the multiple goals implied by multiple-use management is given by Bell (1976).

The advantage of these models for practical application is that the mathematical basis need never become obtrusive.   It is easy to understand that the first task in finding a solution to an optimisation problem is to find any solution which is feasible.   Having found a feasible solution, we then seek an improvement and continue seeking further improvements until we are sure that we are at (or very close to) the optimum.   Precisely how this is done need not concern the practical user and does not detract from the value or understanding of the model.   Instead, those concerned with land-use planning are free to concentrate on the really important questions of defining the objectives of land use and the constraints.   Great precision is not needed in the original definition and formulation of either the objective function or the constraints.   Every solution of a mathematical programming model gives two results, namely the values of the xs which maximise the objective function and the constraint which needs to be relaxed to give an even better solution.   It is, therefore, preferable to work sequentially towards a definition

of the problem which is agreed by all the agencies taking part in the land-use assessment, through a series of workshops.   The resulting policy is developed from a
frank declaration of the conflicts of the separate policies of the agencies, and is
developed as a feasible compromise.   Furthermore, working with a model of this kind
greatly simplifies and clarifies the discussion between the agencies, as there is
little point in discussing the precise formulation or trade-off of any particular
constraint until it has been shown to be limiting.   This interactive use of the
model, by the administrator or policy-maker, like hanging, *concentrates his mind
wonderfully* (Johnson, 1977)!

Experience with the application of dynamic modelling to land-use assessment is now
being developed at a variety of different scales, from English counties and regions
made up of several counties, to larger areas such as the whole of the British uplands or the northern desert ecosystems of Egypt.   As yet, relatively little of
this experience has been published, but a structure plan working paper issued
jointly by Cumbria County Council and the Lake District Special Planning Board
(Bunce and Smith, 1978) describes analyses used to provide the information for the
choice of land-use strategies in Cumbria.   The paper provides the basic document
on which future monitoring and extensions to the analytical work will be built.

The Cumbria model began with an ecological survey in which basic land forms were
separated from the superficial features superimposed upon them.   A preliminary
classification of 1 km squares was derived from a multivariate analysis of attributes obtained from an 11 per cent sample of all km squares on Ordnance Survey maps
of the county.   This analysis was used to assign the remaining 89 per cent of
squares in the county to the classes, showing well-defined patterns of distribution
within the county that relate well to known geomorphological features, but which
also show interesting patterns not readily apparent from direct observation.

A further sample of squares was visited for the purposes of surveying the vegetation.
Analysis of these data gave clearly-defined types of vegetation that were strongly
and significantly associated with the land classes.   The high correlations between
land class and vegetation made it possible to predict the vegetation composition of
vegetation of those squares which had not been visited but where the land class was
known.

Finally, by the use of linear programming, it was possible to examine a range of
alternative policies, with various combinations of objectives, management options
and fixed land-use patterns.   For example, three policy options were explored within fixed land-use constraints in the national parks, the proposed North Pennines
Area of Outstanding Natural Beauty and common land.   A land-use pattern was produced
to maximise the production of timber and keep other outputs at least at their present
levels.

Similarly, the land-use patterns which maximised meat production and which maximised
food energy were also produced.   Such analyses, and the maps derived from them,
can provide a basis for the derivation of policies for rural areas when the social
and economic factors are considered against priorities for planned change in the way
land is to be used.   These analyses assume a particular importance when land-use
policies have to be viewed against major changes such as shortages of fossil fuels,
chronic unemployment, economic recession and a world timber shortage.

Experience with the application of optimisation techniques to data on land-use assessment suggests the following conclusions:

1. Land use involves many agencies and interests, with conflicting policies, which
are not always fully aware of the nature and extent of the conflicts.

2. while some of the constraints to optimum land use (e.g., altitude, soil type and

geographical disaggregation) cannot be relaxed, there are many constraints which are capable of either relaxation or modification.

3. It is important to generate the widest possible range of feasible solutions rather than to select the best of a limited number of possible solutions.

4. It is essential to begin the discussion and search for an acceptable land-use strategy as early as possible in the process of land assessment in order to prevent the taking of entrenched positions which make rational discussion impossible.

5. Areas of future research and collection of improved data are more quickly identified as the problems of land-use allocation are defined and bounded, leading to increased economy of research and field survey.

These conclusions lead to three basic questions about the future of land capability assessment in Scotland.   First, are we going to attempt an integrated land-use policy for Scotland as a result of all the work which has been described at this symposium?   Second, if we are going to derive such a policy, who in Scotland will take the responsibility for co-ordinating the many kinds of research, survey and analysis that will be necessary?   Third, which organisation, capable of standing independent from the various agencies advocating policies, will undertake the analysis and review of the policy options against the background knowledge and the dynamic modelling of the land-use assessment?   We need the answers to these questions urgently, because we should have started on this work yesterday!

REFERENCES

Batty, M. (1972). Recent Developments in land use modelling : a review of British research.   *Urban Studies 9*, 151-177.

Bell, E.F. (1976). *Goal Programming for Land Use Planning*.   USDA For.Serv.,Gen. Tech.Rep. PNW-53.

Bunce, R.G.H. and R.S. Smith (1978). *An Ecological Survey of Cumbria*.   Structure Working Plan Paper 4.   Cumbria County Council/Lake District Special Planning Board, Kendal.

Canada Land Inventory (1970). *Objectives, Scope and Organisation*.   Rep. 1, 2nd edn.

Converse, A.O. (1970). *Optimization*.   Holt, Rinehart & Winston, New York.

Gifford, D. (1971). Comment.   *Bulletin, British Ecological Society, 2*, 2.

Greenberg, M.R. (1978). *Applied Linear Programming for the Socio-Economic and Environmental Sciences*.   Academic Press, London & New York.

Hoos, Ida R. (1972). *Systems analysis in public policy - a critique*.   University of California Press, California.

Jeffers, J.N.R. (1976). Future prospects of systems analysis in ecology.   In G.W. Arnold & C.T. de Wit (Eds), *Critical Evaluation of Systems Analysis in Ecosystems Research and Management,* 98-108.   Pudoc, Wageningen.

Jeffers, J.N.R. (1979). *The Development of Models in Urban and Regional Planning*. In press.

Johnson, S. (1777). Letter to Boswell.   In: *Life of Johnson,* by Boswell, vol.iii, 167.

Kenjins, P.M. (1974). An application of linear programming methodology for regional strategy making, *Regional Studies 8*, 267-279.

Swartzman, G.L. and G.M. Van Dyne (1972). An ecologically based simulation-optimization approach to natural resource planning, *Ann. Rev. Ecology & Systematics 3*, 347-398.

Walters, C.J. (1975). *Foreclosure of Options in Sequential Resource Development Decisions,* IIASA Res. Rep. RR-75-12.

DISCUSSION

Comment by T.J. Maxwell, Hill Farming Research Organisation, Penicuik.

Perhaps I am not the most appropriate person to lead a discussion on this paper because I did not require to be convinced of the usefulness of the techniques Mr. Jeffers is suggesting; my colleagues and I have already attempted to use the technique
to examine land use with respect to agriculture and forestry.   I find myself in considerable agreement with much of what Mr. Jeffers has presented in his paper, and
therefore I will be guilty of reiterating much of what he has said.

Perhaps the most important feature of the method presented is a recognition of the
fact that objectives have to be clearly defined, and the constraints involved in achieving these objectives have to be explicitly stated.   The relentless logic required
by any form of modelling avoids or draws attention to ambiguity; it demands expression of the frequently inarticulated prejudices of those involved in decision making.
It is perhaps the fact that modelling demands a level and vigour of thinking which
many people find too painful to undertake that has prevented the development of its
wider use and application in decision making.   Instead it seems that we continue to
rely on intuitive processes and vague statements about objectives and constraints.
If the technique is to be useful I would reiterate Mr. Jeffers' suggestion that much
more will have to be done quickly.

Mr. Jeffers uses a phrase in his abstract the *full potential of land use*.   Do we
have any clear idea about the complexity involved in realising the *full potential
of land use;* indeed, is it a concept that can be defined?   What range of objectives
have to be considered and how can we determine what these objectives ought to be?
Presumably we have to determine this from society at some stage and it is important
in this respect to recognise that objectives will become clearer after a land use
assessment has been carried out.   In other words the process is cyclical and dynamic
modelling has much to offer in determining not only means but also the ends.   By
recognising this I believe we will avoid the potential hazard that Mr. Jeffers has
alluded to, *that groups will take up entrenched positions which make rational discussion impossible.*

The decision making process at the point at which the *ephemeral* constraints have to
be applied becomes complex.   It is perhaps worth making the point, though it may
be that it is implicitly understood, that the political, aesthetic and economic constraints which presumably reflect the nature of society's desires may turn out to be
far more important than any of the attributes which determine the physical output
from land.

Earlier Coppock commented on objectives in terms of need and how they had grown
piecemeal, depending on the provisions for change, the political strength of vested
interests, changing views about conservation and development, political goals and
philosophies, and accidents of personalities and events.   It seems to me that this
is an accurate description of how things are and are likely to be.   However, I believe that an informed society will increasingly demand to know, in explicit and
unequivocal terms why certain decisions about land use are being taken.

The approach outlined by Mr. Jeffers seems to me to offer considerable potential
for providing the necessary background to making informed and better decisions about
land use and ultimately enabling society to be better informed about the changes
that are necessary to meet its needs and objectives.

There is however a continuing need to be clear about the nature of constraints - how
real are they?   Do they merely reflect the preconceived notions about a limited
number of objectives and therefore inevitably result in the achievement of these objectives.   Viewed more realistically many changes can be made which release us from

these constraints making it possible for a much wider range of objectives to be met.

Our own limited experience and application of the technique to the use of land as between forestry and agriculture has led us to the conclusion that both activities can contribute more to society than they may do separately but such solutions are likely to require changes in the accepted management operations and constraints of both forestry and agriculture.

As to the need for future research and the priority given to certain aspects of re-search, dynamic modelling can give a much clearer identification of those aspects which require attention.   What is also required, however, is the flexibility in research programmes and adaptability among researchers to take account of those matters which deserve attention.

Comment by C.E. Chulvick, University of Edinburgh.

How practical is it to assume that decision-makers will accept an optimization model? There is evidence to the contrary in the attempt of the DOE to dissuade planners from using mathematical models and the lack of success of the *Alternative Futures* technique in the U.S. in the 1970s.

CHAPTER 12

POSTSCRIPT - ASSESSING LAND FOR SCOTLAND'S FUTURE

M.F. Thomas
Department of Earth and Environmental Science,
University of Stirling

ABSTRACT

Existing systems of land assessment reveal disagreements about objectives and lack of
agreement on methodology. Collection and handling of environmental data pose problems of selection, scale, time and cost. Scale of survey should be appropriate to
scale of land management, and techniques should be sensitive to landform configuration
and its relations with climate and soil. Acquisition of new environmental data is
considered as important as the development of new systems of analysis. Wider consultation and agreement on methodology should lead to greater investment of resources
for land research in Scotland.

KEYWORDS

Land classification; survey methodology; mapping scale; environmental data acquisition; land unit boundaries; geomorphology in land research; consultation on research priorities.

The respect which a country has for its land can perhaps be measured by the allocation of national resources to its appraisal, development and protection. In the
United Kingdom the resources available for scientific research into land quality and
performance under different uses remain meagre, when measured against the size and
complexity of the task. Jeffers (Ch. 11) rightly points out that sectional interests continue to follow separate lines of investigation and to satisfy often conflicting aims or divergent objectives. Nevertheless, it has been possible at this Symposium to bring together most of those organisations actively engaged in land assessment in Scotland, and it is evident that many recognise their common needs and the
merits of close technical co-operation. It was even suggested to the organisers
that it would scarcely be possible to hold such a meeting to cover the same topic for
England and Wales. Does this indicate that we have made greater progress in this
field of enquiry in Scotland, or merely that factors of scale and geography favour
co-operative ventures? It is probable that we must accept the latter proposition,
but if this is correct, it must surely be a reason for optimism for future work on
land assessment, even if the present level of understanding gives no reason for com-
placency.

One problem with any co-ordinated and comprehensive scheme of land evaluation, is
that many people will see such an exercise as a major stop towards rigid land-use
planning, rather than as a foundation for taking national decisions on land use, at

any level from the private landholder to the regional planner or national development agency.   Yet, by avoiding this issue a country does not avoid planning; it simply invites bad planning.   A more serious and recurrent question is whether objective land assessment is possible, except with respect to a particular land use carried out under specified conditions.   But although this question invariably receives unsatisfactory answers, it is perhaps the wrong question to pose in the first place.

There are clearly several different approaches to these problems.   By assuming that agriculture, and particularly arable agriculture, should be the major focus of attention on surviving rural land, it has proved possible to produce maps of Agricultural Land Classification (MAFF, 1974; DAFS, 1976) for the entire country and to apply a scheme of Land Use Capability Classification (Bibby and Mackney, 1969) for selected areas covered by detailed soil surveys.

Such attempts which have many antecedents do not command universal approval.   In his introduction to this volume Coppock notes that Hilton (1968) emphasised the importance of economic appraisals of land.   Hilton (1968) also thought that land classified according to inherent physical characteristics should remain ungraded on final maps. Boddington (1978) complains that the absence of a second, economic, stage of land classification robs the scheme of much of its utility, particularly for urban planners. The ranking of land according to limitations gives little regard to versatility or to the productive potential of the land under the most suitable crop and management. Boddington (1978) also recalls Vink's (1960) comment that *all good land classification is based on a good soil classification* and notes that published data in this field do not permit precise parameters of land quality to be mapped at a local level.

How little we really know about the upland environments of Britain is all too evident. The work co-ordinated by Stamp (1948) in the 1930s and 1940s is regarded by Boddington (1978) as superior in many respects to the Agricultural Land Classification of 1974, while Locke (Ch. 6) reveals that the Forestry Commission used this source to identify *heathland, moorland* and *rough grazing* for potential afforestation (Fig. 6.1).   These divisions were presumably largely derived in turn from Ordnance Survey maps of the time.   It is worth recalling that when writing on the Classification of Land in 1960 Stamp noted the complexity of the problem and stressed that the modern soil map *does not furnish the whole answer to the development of land* (104), and further that a *classification of "types" of land was needed, since what is the "best" land for one purpose is not necessarily the best for another* (106).

In another recent symposium on *The Future of Upland Britain* (Tranter, 1978), Ball indicates that a national map of soil is available only at a scale of 1:1 million, and in the same volume Hill and Evans (1978) record the slow progress towards a national vegetation survey.   In Scotland the work of the Soil Survey for Scotland discussed in Chapter 3 by Bibby indicates many of the problems of covering large areas of upland Scotland to produce soil maps at a scale of 1:250,000.   The situation is in fact even worse, for Francis points out (Ch. 4) that the choice of appropriate parameters of climate is still uncertain.   The selection of such parameters clearly exercised Birse and his colleagues (Birse and others, 1970, 1971) in the preparation of their maps of *climatic resources* for Scotland.   But here their major problem was the lack of meteorological records for the Scottish Highlands, and their maps (as Francis notes) include a high degree of topographic extrapolation.   It is also important to recognise that these maps relate specifically to Scottish conditions and offer no direct basis for comparison with the climates of the rest of the United Kingdom.

The argument that there is little need for detailed survey of the bleak highland areas of Scotland is belied by the requirements of most users of the uplands.   Locke (Ch. 6) emphasises the importance of local landform and soil patterns to planting programmes.   Such patterns must also be important for all upland management, though the most appropriate scale may vary.   In the area of nature conservation interest

attaches to specific sites.   It is noticeable that throughout this volume the importance of local scale in land assessment is repeated, mainly in the context of the influence of landform pattern (for instance, on soil properties), local climate, and
accessibility.   Such information cannot usually be displayed at scales smaller than
1:50,000, and may be required at larger scales (up to 1:10,000).   Provision of information at this level requires the acquisition of new field data for most upland areas,
and is demanding in terms of investment of time and skill by experienced scientists.
The excellent new 1:10,000 maps of the Ordnance Survey offer a unique store of topographic and much other data, for instance, but the abstraction of these data from the
eventual total number (about 4,000 sheets) for Scotland would be a task of great magnitude and would raise questions about method in relation to precision and cost of
surveys (Beckett, 1968).

From these observations many different conclusions are possible, but two central questions concerning methodology for future land assessment stand out.   The first concerns
the collection, storage and handling of environmental and ecological data;   the second
concerns the grading of land for various uses.   Because of its complexity, the latter
problem may appear the more difficult to solve, but in reality the two are closely
linked.   Maps of agricultural land classification reveal little about the inherent
characteristics of the land on which they must be based, and therefore there must
be loss of information which cannot then be applied to alternative land uses.   Maps
of Land Use Capability which arise from soil surveys present more environmental data
and Boddington (1978) advocates their wider use.   In Scotland this seems likely to
come about from the present programme.   Yet, in Chapter 1, Coppock voices the widespread concern over the value of any single rating of Capability for parcels of land,
when different land uses may require quite separate appraisals, as has been appreciated
in the Canada Land Inventory (CLI, 1968).

It may thus be argued that since field data are expensive and sometimes difficult to
obtain;   may not always be appropriate to unforeseen land uses;   and may even be based
on poor understanding of the ecological relationships present in the existing landscape, we should not proceed to acquire such environmental data for their own sake.
But there are serious difficulties in this view.   When decisions about land use have
to be taken they must usually be considered quickly, and it is scarcely possible then
to go out and collect relevant data.   They must mostly be available and in a suitable
form from the outset.   The acquisition of data and their presentation in the most
useful form are therefore major issues.

The preparation of Land Use Capability maps is an example of what Bunce, Morrell and
Stel (1975, 153) describe as a *classification by direct observation and interpretation
of ground features* which proceeds to the interpretation of pattern before undertaking
analysis.   These authors also level this criticism at early attempts at ecological
mapping undertaken in Canada by Hills (1961), who has recently re-stated principles
for an holistic approach to ecological land classification (Hills, 1978), and the
Braun-Blanquet school of phytosociology which has been developed to deal with land
evaluation (Long, 1974).   The alternative offered by Bunce and his colleagues at
the Institute of Terrestrial Ecology (ITE) is the multivariate analysis of available
environmental data (Bunce and others, 1975) which is closely linked with systems modelling advocated by Jeffers (Ch. 11).   It is claimed that classificatory procedures
embodied in these methods allow for a strategy of minimum effective field sampling
which is mainly based upon an Indicator Species Analysis.

This work has used the Ordnance Survey grid for sampling purposes and involved the
extraction of basic data from the 1:50,000 (or 1:63,360) Ordnance Survey maps.   The
pilot study of Grizedale used 12 variables from 0.5 x 0.5 km squares.   Of these variables, 3 concerned altitude, 2 location, 6 relative distances from various features,
and 1 the extent of woodland (Bunce and others, 1975).   When this technique was extended to the whole of Cumbria for the County Council (Bunce and Smith, 1978) a 1 x
1 km square was used and 186 variables employed of which 152 were derived from the

1:63,360 map.   This analysis led to the discrimination of 16 land classes.   A further desk study for the whole of England and Wales produced 8 national classes of upland land from 51 variables within 10 x 10 km squares (Heal, 1976).   The Agricultural Land Classification for England and Wales places all the upland into classes 4 and 5, and even the more sensitive Land Use Capability Classification provides only classes 5 - 7.   It is suggested that these groupings provide too little discrimination between different types of upland (Heal, 1976).

Doubts about the application of these methods must arise when it is recognised that no specific soil data were included in the survey of Cumbria (Bunce and Smith, 1978) and that the study of England and Wales reduced 71 soil mapping units to 7 in the ITE data store (Ball, 1978).   Data of unequal ecological significance appear to be accepted without selection or weighting.   Sophisticated analyses are thus performed on an array of data already available from published sources, usually Ordnance Survey and Geological Maps, but not always from Soil Maps which have not been prepared for all areas, especially in the uplands.   We can, however, learn a salutary lesson from this work that such maps contain a great store of information which we often ignore or have previously considered inaccessible, although Stamp (1950) was able to draw on such data in the 1930s and 1940s to produce 10 Land Potential Classes.   It was also found that there is a strong interdependence between human and environmental systems and that *the map classification was strongly correlated with biological systems that were present on the ground* (Bunce and others, 163) and that *the overriding influence of altitude* (164) probably accounted for the strength of many correlations.

However, there are yet some drawbacks to this approach.   The 1 km square is internally complex and Bunce and colleagues (1975, 165) consider that *the classification of squares needs to be reassessed at a scale involving landforms*.   But this is no easy task, and it still begs the question of scale since landforms themselves can be analysed at different scales.   It is clear from many of the papers in this volume that problems frequently arise at the local scale, that is to say at the level of land management, and at this scale the characteristics of landform frequently dominate the total environmental complex.   Landforms, particularly in upland areas, tend to provide the boundaries for environmental or ecological units, and it is this question of boundaries which the use of grid squares for ease of multivariate analysis cannot yet solve.   However, a similar study undertaken by the ITE for Shetland (see Milner, 1978) drew on a wide range of source material including aerial photography and produced maps sensitive to surface configuration (Experimental Cartography Unit, 1978).

The problems of scale and of the mapping or search for natural land units are on the other hand addressed directly by many techniques of soil survey.   In addition to field survey this work tends to draw more on air photo interpretation and the use of other techniques of remote sensing than on the abstraction of conventional map data (Lawrence and others, 1977).   The work of the Macaulay Institute, illustrated by Bibby (Ch. 3) is centrally concerned with these questions, but they are by no means new.   Nearly all agencies concerned with land mapping and classification have confronted these problems (see Thomas, 1976).   In the 1950s the Division of Land Research in Australia developed the Land System and Land Unit (Christian and Stewart, 1957), while in the 1960s Beckett and Webster (1965) worked on the Land Facet and Recurrent Landscape Pattern.   Such was the international interest in these units at this time that a working group attempted to formalise an hierarchy of land units at different scales (Brink and others, 1966).   In Canada, Hills (1961) had already advanced a system for ecological mapping and in that country research, first for the Canada Land Inventory and more recently by the Canada Committee on Ecological Land Classification (CCELC) has actively continued this work.   The first major set of papers issued by the CCELC,(Thie and Ironside, 1976) illustrates these issues.   Hierarchic schemes of land units have occasioned much theoretical debate in both eastern and western Europe as well as in Australia, Canada and elsewhere (see, for instance, Prokayev, 1962;   Isachenko, 1965;   Rowe, 1961, 1976;   Hertz, 1973;   Tricart, 1973; Wright, 1972;   Thomas, 1976;   Dansereau and Pare, 1976).   Although the discussions have been inconclusive in respect of theory, the use of land mapping units in soil and related surveys continues, and because boundaries are necessary to all land users and indeed to all land planners, the search for the most appropriate boundaries remains of practical concern.

The geomorphological basis of most attempts to delimit boundaries is widely recognised, and has been acknowledged in much of the work quoted.   Writers in this volume have repeatedly referred to the importance of landforms or landform attributes.   Yet, as Snaydon (1978, 679) states in his summing up of discussions by the conservation and ecology group at the symposium on *The Future of Upland Britain*, *physiography and geomorphology are not sufficiently considered* and more intensive mapping is required. It has also been noted by Boddington (1978) and in this volume that insufficient knowledge of climate hinders rational land assessment.

It therefore appears that the ITE system (Bunce and others, 1975, 1978) is one that relies heavily on the strong correlation between land attributes, especially in an area such as Cumbria and allows the use of surrogate data from Ordnance Survey maps to replace a fuller understanding of the environment which could arise from new field survey.   By using a grid to facilitate the manipulation of data, the ITE system has so far not only lacked a level of resolution which would allow boundaries to be drawn around natural land units, but it also specifically excludes the recognition or mapping of these units from field survey or from remote sensing imagery.   It is only by the inclusion of a vegetation survey that the system is tied directly to ecological data, though the sample taken was small (48 1 km squares to represent 7,100 squares in Cumbria).

It is not the intention to underestimate the value of new techniques for handling data.   It is clear from the papers presented here that several organisations have recognised the need for data banks and information systems, and ITE points the way to the more efficient use of these systems.   Yet, in any consideration of the future of land assessment in Scotland, it is scarcely possible to consider this approach sufficient in itself.   It is possibly important to note that the Canada Geographic Information System (CGIS, 1973) which is based on the Canada Land Inventory (CLI, 1970) data was designed to accept mapped field data in the form of unit boundaries, using a drum scanner.   In this way data can be handled with respect to land units as an alternative, or in addition, to the use of grid squares.

Many of the boundaries required for land classification can be derived from the products of remote sensing.   The conventional panchromatic aerial photograph is, of course, widely used in soil and other land surveys, to provide a stereoscopic model of the terrain from which boundaries can be drawn for subsequent checking in the field.   What is very noticeable in the contributions to this volume is that the appraisal and use of remote sensing techniques in the field of land assessment remains ancillary or experimental.   Kirby (Ch. 2) refers to the meteorological disadvantages of Scotland where the acquisition of data by remote sensing is concerned, but, not withstanding our adverse weather conditions, progress in this field has been totally inadequate.   Why is it that infra-red, multi-band and radar imagery remain experimental, and true colour photography is available only for special areas such as the coastal zones?   The Natural Environment Research Council (NERC) carried out experimental remote sensing flights using multi-spectral photography in 1971 (Curtis and Mayer, 1974), but this was not designed for land assessment purposes and the work does not appear to have been extended.   Many developing countries have acquired, through aid programmes, high-quality remotely-sensed imagery.   Sierra Leone, for instance, has a national coverage of high resolution colour infra-red aerial photography.   The mosaics of existing aerial photography for Scotland, of different dates and scales (Figs. 2.1-2.4), and the general absence of colour and colour infra-red coverage, are witness to the low priority given to the acquisition of this type of material.

Early Landsat (1 and 2) pictures had a low resolution (80 sq m) and even the high resolution RBV images from Landsat 3 (Kirby, Ch. 2) are restricted to pixels of 24m^2 dimensions which may preclude their use for detailed land assessment.   Nevertheless both satellite and radar imagery certainly possess great potential for monitoring the environment of upland (and lowland) Scotland.

It is also important to add that new techniques of abstracting data from photographic imagery are also available to supplement the more intuitive air-photo interpretation, and a considerable literature is now devoted to this question which cannot be explored here.   In the United Kingdom we have too often been complacent, sceptical or even dismissive of this range of new sources of data.

Many of the points made here are fundamentally a question of the allocation of na-tional resources.   It would be a mistake to spend large sums on the storage and computer modelling of existing data, without a parallel recognition of the need to acquire new environmental data from remote sensing, ground recording, and field mapping.   If too little account has been taken of geomorphology as a dominant set of influences on other land patterns, it is equally true that, despite the important and innovative work of the Institute of Hydrology and the Meteorological Office, the poor coverage of ground recording stations in upland Britain places a fundamental limitation on the assessment of its climatic resources (Birse and others, 1970, 1971).

In some respects we still lack confidence in these fields; confidence that boundaries drawn from landforms will be valid for other distributions, and that measured para-meters of climate or of soil properties will be relevant to as yet unstated land-use options.   Thus we have to decide the question Coppock poses, whether surveys of national land resources are sufficiently beneficial to justify their high cost. They should be, if only because questions about the future use of land frequently arise in contexts that demand decisions to be taken at short notice.   The acquisi-tion of environmental data is a long-term process, and the nation should prepare as much as possible in advance to provide the basis for answers to questions concerning the future use of its land resources.

The conclusions here that much necessary environmental information is not available, that more intensive field mapping is required, that information storage and retrieval are central issues, were all identified by Snaydon (1978) at the recent Symposium in Reading.   They point to the need for the allocation of a greater share of national resources to the study of land as the country's most basic natural resource.

Jeffers (Ch. 11) asks who will co-ordinate research, be responsible for future policy, and for the revision of options in an integrated land-use policy.   In the field of environmental research the current level of co-ordination appears to leave many ques-tions unanswered.   We do not appear to possess a structure within Scotland or more widely in the United Kingdom, which can assess the claims of different methodologies for land research, and sift the priorities for fund allocation.   It is also true, as Davidson points out in his comment on Bibby's paper (Ch. 3), that little account is taken of progress overseas in this field.   There is no doubt that Scotland has particular environmental characteristics and disadvantages which need specific en-quiry, but the matter of land assessment is a question of lively debate in most ad-vanced countries.   It is also a concern of many branches of science.   At this, still formative stage in land research in Scotland it should be an urgent priority to assess the options open in terms of research method, and this has of course to be viewed in relation to a set of stated objectives.   Such an appraisal will require a wider consultation between different institutions and environmental scientists. If this were done and a broad measure of agreement reached then the allocation of greater resources to land research could be justified as vital to the nation's future.

REFERENCES

Ball, D.F., (1978). The soils of upland Britain.   In R.B. Tranter (Ed), *The Future of Upland Britain*, vol. II. Centre for Agricultural Strategy, Pap. 2, Univ. Reading, 397–416.

Beckett, P.H.T. and R. Webster, (1965). *A Classification System for Terrain*. Military Eng. Exptl. Establishment, Rep. *872*, Christchurch, U.K.

Beckett, P.H.T., (1968). Method and scale of land resource surveys in relation to precision and cost.   In G.A. Stewart (Ed), *Land Evaluation*, Macmillan, Melbourne, 53–63.

Bibby, J.S., (1973). Land capability.   In J. Tivy (Ed), *The Organic Resources of Scotland*, Oliver and Boyd, Edinburgh, 51–65.

Bibbsy, J.S. and D. Mackney, (1969). *Land Use Capability Classification*.   Tech. Monogr. 1 Soil Surv. Gt. Br., Harpenden.

Birse, E.L. and F.T. Dry, (1970). *Assessment of Climatic Conditions in Scotland*. 1 Based on accumulated temperature and potential water deficit.   Macaulay Inst. Soil Res., Aberdeen.

Birse, E.L. and L. Robertson, (1970). *Assessment of Climatic Conditions in Scotland*. 2 Based on exposure and accumulated frost.   Macaulay Inst. Soil Res., Aberdeen.

Birse, E.L., (1971). *Assessment of Climatic Conditions in Scotland*. 3 The Bioclimatic sub-regions.   Macaulay Inst. Soil Res., Aberdeen.

Boddington, M.A.B., (1978). *The Classification of Agricultural Land in England and Wales : a Critique*.   Rural Planning Services, Publ. 4.

Brink, A.B., J.A. Mabbutt, R. Webster and P.H.T. Beckett, (1966). *Report of the Working Group on Land Classification and Data Storage*.   Military Eng. Exptl. Est. Rep. *940*, Christchurch, U.K.

Brinkmann, R. and A.J. Smyth, (1973). *Land Evaluation for Rural Purposes*.   Int. Inst. for Land Reclamation and Improvement/ILRI, Publ. *17*, Wageningen, Netherlands.

Bunce, R.G.H., S.K. Morrell and H. Stel, (1975). The application of multivariate analysis to regional survey.   *J. Env. Management*, 3, 151–56.

Bunce, R.G.H. and R.S. Smith, (1978). *An Ecological Survey of Cumbria*.   Cumbria County Council and Lake District. Spec. Planning Bd., Working Pap. *4*, Kendal.

Canada Geographic Information System, (1973). *Canada Geographic Information System : Overview*.   Lands Directorate, Ottawa.

Canada Land Inventory, (1970). *The Canada Land Inventory : Objectives, Scope and Organisation*.   The Canada Land Inventory Rep. *1*, Ottawa.

Curtis, L.F. and A.E.S. Mayer, (1974). *Remote Sensing Evaluation Flights 1971*.   Nat. Env. Res. Council, Publ., Ser. C, *12*.

Dansereau, P. and G. Pare, (1977). *Ecological Grading and Classification of Land Occupation and Land-Use Mosaics*.   Geogrl. Pap. *58*, Lands Directorate, Ottawa.

Experimental Cartography Unit, (1978). Maps from the Shetland Data Bank.   *Geogrl. Mag.*, *50*, 736–53.

Heal, O.W., (1977). Upland land use.   In *Inst. Terrestrial Ecol. Ann. Rep. 1976*, HMSO, London, 10–15.

Hertz, K., (1973). Beitrag zur Theorie der landschafts-analytischen Masstabsbereiche *Petermanns Geogr. Mitt.*, *117*, 91–96.

Hill, M.O. and D.F. Evans, (1978). The vegetation of upland Britain.   In R.B. Tranter (Ed), *The Future of Upland Britain Vol., II*.   Centre for Agricultural Strategy, Pap. 2, Univ. Reading, 397–416.

Hills, G.A., (1961). *The Ecological Basis of Land-Use Planning*.   Ontario Dept. Lands and Forests, Res. Rep. *46*, Toronto.

Hills, G.A., (1976). An integrated iterative holistic approach to ecosystem classification.   In J. Thie and G. Ironside (Eds). *Ecological (Biophysical) Land Classification in Canada*.   Ecol. Land. Class, Ser. *1*, 73–98.

Hilton, N., (1968). An approach to agricultural land classification in Great Britain. *Land Use and Resources : Studies in Applied Geography*, Inst. Br. Geographers, Spec. Publ. *1*, 127–42.

Isachenko, A.G., (1965). *Principles of Landscape Science and Physical Geographic Regionalisation*.   Engl. Tranl. R.J. Zatorski, edited J.S. Massey (1973), Melbourne U.P.

Long, G., (1974). *Diagnostic Phyto-ecologique et Amenagement du Territoire 1 : Principes Generaux et Methodes*.   Coll. Ecol., Masson et Cie, Paris.

Milner, C., (1978). Shetland ecology surveyed.   *Geogrl. Mag., 50*, 730-36.

Ministry of Agriculture, Fisheries and Food, Agricultural Development and Advisory Service, (1974). *Agricultural Land Classification*.   MAFF Tech. Rep. *11*, HMSO, London.

Prokayev, V.I., (1962). The facies as the basic and smallest unit in landscape science *Soviet Geog., 3*, 21-29.

Rowe, J.S., (1961). The level of integration concept and ecology.   *Ecology 42*, 420-27.

Rowe, J.S., (1977). *Working paper, June 1977*.   Canada Committee on Ecological Land Classification.   Working Group on Methodology/Philosophy, Mimeo.

Rowe, J.S., (1978). personal communication.

Snaydon, R.W., (1978). Points from papers : conservation and ecology group.   In R.B. Tranter (Ed). *The Future of Upland Britain*.   *Vol. II*, Centre for Agricultural Strategy, CAS Paper 2, Univ. Reading, App. 1:7, 679-81.

Stamp, L.D., (1948). The classification of land.   In L.D. Stamp (Ed). *The Land of Britain its Use and Misuse. 2 edtn.*, Longmans, London.

Stamp, L.D., (1960). *Applied Geography*, Penguin Books, Harmondsworth.

Thomas, M.F., (1976). Purpose, scale and method in land resource surveys.   *Geographia Polonica 34*, 207-23.

Tricart, J., (1973). La geomorphologie dans les etudes integres d'amenagement du milieu naturel.   *Ann. Geog. 82*, 421-53.

Vink, A.P.A., (1960). Quantitative aspects of land classification.   *Trans. 7th Int. Cong. Soil Sci. IV*, Madison.

Wright, R.L., (1972). Principles in a geomorphological approach to land classification *Z. Geomorph. N.F. 16*, 351-73.